Grammar Toolkit Lesson Plans for Middle School

Grammar Toolkit Lesson Plans for Middle School: Mentor Text-Based Grammar Lessons for the Middle School English Classroom contains detailed grammar lesson plans for teachers in grades six, seven, and eight. The lesson plans in this book incorporate the research-based best practices of grammar instruction. They present grammatical concepts in the context of effective writing through the use of mentor texts. These mentor text examples, which students read from a writer's perspective, deepen students' metacognition of the importance of these concepts and help them see the elements of grammar as tools for strong writing that authors use strategically to make their work as strong as possible. The thorough plans in this book are designed to help teachers put the best practices of grammar instruction into action in their teaching in concrete, practitioner-oriented ways that are informed by key research findings on the teaching of grammar. The ideas, examples, and instructional suggestions in this book will give teachers the necessary resources to incorporate mentor-text-based grammar lessons that develop students' metacognition of the tools of effective grammar and communication.

Sean Ruday (he/him/his) is a professor and program coordinator of English education at Longwood University.

Also Available from Routledge Eye On Education
(www.routledge.com/eyeoneducation)

Grammar Inquiries, Grades 6–12:
An Inquiry- and Asset-Based Approach to Grammar Instruction
Sean Ruday

The Middle School Grammar Toolkit:
Using Mentor Texts to Teach Standards-Based Language and Grammar in Grades 6–8, 2nd edition
Sean Ruday

Student-Centered Literacy Assessment in the 6–12 Classroom:
An Asset-Based Approach
Sean Ruday and Katie Caprino

Remote Teaching and Learning in the Middle and High ELA Classroom: Instructional Strategies and Best Practices
Sean Ruday and Jennifer Cassidy

The Narrative Writing Toolkit:
Using Mentor Texts in Grades 3–8
Sean Ruday

The Multimedia Writing Toolkit: Helping Students Incorporate Graphics and Videos for Authentic Purposes, Grades 3–8
Sean Ruday

The First-Year English Teacher's Guidebook: Strategies for Success
Sean Ruday

Culturally Relevant Teaching in the English Language Arts Classroom:
A Guide for Teachers
Sean Ruday

Inquiry-Based Literature Instruction in the 6–12 Classroom:
A Hands-on Guide for Deeper Learning
Sean Ruday and Katie Caprino

Grammar Toolkit Lesson Plans for Middle School

Mentor Text-Based Grammar Lessons for the Middle School English Classroom

Sean Ruday

Routledge
Taylor & Francis Group
NEW YORK AND LONDON

Designed cover image: © Getty Images

First published 2025
by Routledge
605 Third Avenue, New York, NY 10158

and by Routledge
4 Park Square, Milton Park, Abingdon, Oxon, OX14 4RN

Routledge is an imprint of the Taylor & Francis Group, an informa business

© 2025 Sean Ruday

The right of Sean Ruday to be identified as author of this work has been asserted in accordance with sections 77 and 78 of the Copyright, Designs and Patents Act 1988.

All rights reserved. The purchase of this copyright material confers the right on the purchasing institution to photocopy or download pages which bear a copyright line at the bottom of the page. No other parts of this book may be reprinted or reproduced or utilised in any form or by any electronic, mechanical, or other means, now known or hereafter invented, including photocopying and recording, or in any information storage or retrieval system, without permission in writing from the publishers.

Trademark notice: Product or corporate names may be trademarks or registered trademarks, and are used only for identification and explanation without intent to infringe.

ISBN: 978-1-032-73947-2 (hbk)
ISBN: 978-1-032-73798-0 (pbk)
ISBN: 978-1-003-46682-6 (ebk)

DOI: 10.4324/9781003466826

Typeset in Palatino
by codeMantra

Access the Support Material: www.routledge.com/9781032737980

Contents

Meet the Author — vii

Introduction: The Power and Possibility of Mentor Text-Based Grammar Lessons — 1

SECTION ONE
Lesson Plans Recommended for the Sixth-Grade English Classroom — 9

Lesson 6.1 The Case of Communication: Pronoun Case — 11

Lesson 6.2 Bringing the Intensity: Intensive Pronouns — 23

Lesson 6.3 Adding and Clarifying: Punctuation that Sets Off Additional Information — 34

Lesson 6.4 Developing and Describing: Adjectives — 45

Lesson 6.5 Explanation and Impact: Adverbs — 55

SECTION TWO
Lesson Plans Recommended for the Seventh-Grade English Classroom — 65

Lesson 7.1 Developing Ideas: Prepositional Phrases — 67

Lesson 7.2 A Descriptive Tool: Relative Clauses — 78

Lesson 7.3 Strong and Specific: Strong Verbs and Specific Nouns — 89

Lesson 7.4 Shades of Meaning: Connotation and Denotation — 100

Lesson 7.5 Intentional Sentence Construction: Simple, Compound, and Complex Sentences — 111

SECTION THREE
Lesson Plans Recommended for the Eighth-Grade English Classroom   123

Lesson 8.1   Purposeful Structures: Active and Passive Voices   125

Lesson 8.2   Time for a Break: Punctuation that Indicates a Pause or Break   135

Lesson 8.3   Key Comparisons: Comparative and Superlative Degrees   147

Lesson 8.4   Tools for Variety and Versatility: Using Verbals   158

Lesson 8.5   The Many Moods: The Indicative, Imperative, Interrogative, Conditional, and Subjunctive Verb Moods   170

SECTION FOUR
Final Thoughts and Resources   181

Conclusion: Using This Book to Maximize Grammar Instruction   183

Appendix A: Annotated Bibliography of Mentor Texts   187
Appendix B: Reproducible Graphic Organizers   193

Note: Appendices A and B are also available online on this book's webpage on the Routledge site (www.routledge.com/9781032737980) for quick and easy access to these resources.

Meet the Author

Sean Ruday (he/him/his) is a professor and program coordinator of English education at Longwood University. He has taught English and language arts in New York, Massachusetts, and Virginia. He holds a BA from Boston College, an MA from New York University, and a PhD from the University of Virginia. Sean is the founding editor of the *Journal of Literacy Innovation*. This is his 18th book with Routledge Eye On Education.

Introduction:
The Power and Possibility of Mentor Text-Based Grammar Lessons

I sat in my office with outstanding young adult and middle-grade novels stacked around me. Works by amazing authors like Jacqueline Woodson, Pablo Cartaya, Renée Watson, Angie Thomas, Jason Reynolds, and more covered my desk and encircled me as I excitedly pounded the keys of my laptop. What was I doing? I was planning lessons on grammar instruction! I was finding examples of key grammatical concepts in these published works, such as adjectives, adverbs, prepositional phrases, relative clauses, and more. For example, I noted the adjective "homemade" in the sentence "I reach for the basket of homemade dinner rolls and pass it" (Watson, 2019, p. 6) from the book *Some Places More Than Others* by Renée Watson. Shortly afterwards, I identified the prepositional phrases "through the woods" and "under my feet" from the sentence "I tiptoe through the woods so the leaves don't crackle under my feet" (Thomas, 2023, p. 2) in Angie Thomas' book *Nic Blake and the Remarkables: The Manifestor Prophecy*. As I found these examples of grammatical concepts, I said to myself, "These examples are going to help students understand grammar in the context of writing. Using them in grammar instruction can help me and other teachers make grammar come alive for students."

This opening anecdote provides a window into how I plan for and think about teaching grammar. When I plan and enact grammar lessons, I incorporate examples from well-written, high-interest, published texts that demonstrate the effective uses of grammatical concepts. These examples are called mentor texts because they guide and mentor students as they learn about writing and how to apply writing strategies to their own works (Dorfman & Cappelli, 2007), connecting their writing experiences to the works of published authors (Marchetti & O'Dell, 2015). In the context of grammar instruction, mentor texts help students understand what key grammatical concepts are, how they are used in effective writing, why they are important to strong writing, and how to apply them to their own works. The lesson plans you'll find in this book represent this approach: they incorporate mentor texts as part of a strategic and intentional process designed to help students understand, use, and reflect on key grammatical concepts that can enhance their own writing, reading, and thinking. In this introductory chapter, we'll explore three concepts related to this book: (1) The best practices of grammar instruction; (2) this book's approach; and (3) what to expect in this book. Let's get started!

The Best Practices of Grammar Instruction

Teaching grammar effectively involves breaking away from some traditional practices and rethinking what grammar instruction can look like. Traditionally, grammar has focused on out-of-context worksheets and activities that are presented separately from student writing (Weaver, 1998). These exercises frequently lead to student disengagement (Wotjer, 1998) and have very little impact on student writing (Weaver, 1998). As teachers, this is exactly what we don't want! If these instructional practices won't make our students better writers and will make them less engaged in their learning, let's use methods that will benefit and resonate with our students!

Research shows that the most effective grammar instruction makes connections to students' experiences with reading and writing (Smagorinsky, 2018), which is often called teaching grammar in context (Anderson, 2005; Weaver, 1998). The question for us as teachers, then, is what is the best way to teach grammar in context? In other words, how can we most effectively teach students about key grammatical concepts, such as those reflected in state and Common Core Standards, while making connections to students' authentic reading and writing experiences? The solution: mentor texts! By studying and discussing how grammatical concepts are used in published texts and the importance of those concepts to the effectiveness of the piece of writing, students can develop deep understandings of what key grammatical concepts are and why they are important (Ruday, 2020). Through the use of mentor texts, students are able to think carefully and thoughtfully about how and why published authors use key grammatical concepts and ways they can apply those same concepts to their own writing.

An especially important benefit of mentor text-based grammar instruction is that it helps students read like writers—by examining the grammatical concepts that authors use, thinking about their importance, and ultimately considering how they can apply those concepts in their own works, students gain a deeper understanding of these concepts than if they only examined them through out-of-context worksheets (Ruday, 2020). In this approach, literature is an entryway to effective grammar instruction; it helps students understand the features and importance of the grammatical concepts they study. The idea of reading like writers is supported by the National Council of Teachers of English (NCTE), which asserts that "writing and reading are related" and recommends that teachers understand "how writers read for the purposes of writing–with an eye toward not just what the text says but how it is put together" (NCTE Professional Knowledge for the Teaching of Writing, 2016, Writing and reading are related section). Teachers can then use this understanding of how writers can engage with texts to help their students read in a similarly purposeful way.

When students examine how a grammatical concept is used in a published mentor text and reflect on its significance, they can enhance their understanding of grammar by increasing their metacognition of it. Metacognition, knowledge of cognitive phenomena (Flavell, 1979), can play an important role in effective grammar instruction (Cook, 2020; Ruday, 2020) by helping students understand why a writer might have chosen to use a particular grammatical concept and what impact that concept might have on the written work. For example, let's take a look at the excerpt from Angie Thomas' (2023) book *Nic Blake and the Remarkables: The Manifestor Prophecy* previously featured in this chapter: "I tiptoe through the woods so the leaves don't crackle under my feet" (p. 2). By reflecting on the importance of the prepositional phrases "through the woods" and "under my feet" and considering why the author may have chosen to include them in their work, students will develop their metacognition of the significance and impact of this concept.

When students think metacognitively about grammatical concepts, they can begin to see them as tools that authors strategically use in writing and not just terms and definitions that need to be memorized. Because of this, I like to explain to students that grammatical concepts function as tools for effective communication that writers intentionally use in their works to maximize its effectiveness (Ruday, 2020). When I do so, I explain that, just as all tools have specific uses and are utilized purposefully based on a certain task or project, grammatical concepts also have particular uses and are best incorporated into writing with clear understandings of how and why to use them. Like we would select a screwdriver if it is the best tool for a specific job, we would also use a prepositional phrase if it's the most effective way to add detail to a text. This toolkit-based approach helps enhance students' metacognition and their abilities to read as writers while helping them learn grammar in the context of authentic reading and writing.

The information in this section has shared key research-based findings and approaches that relate to effective grammar instruction. Based on these ideas, five especially important guidelines for teaching grammar are:

1. Teach grammar in the context of reading and writing.
2. Incorporate mentor texts.
3. Show students how to read like writers.
4. Develop students' metacognition of grammatical concepts.
5. Talk with students about how grammatical concepts are tools for effective writing.

Now, let's explore this book's approach and its connection to the best practices of grammar instruction.

This Book's Approach

The lesson plans in this book incorporate the research-based best practices of grammar instruction. They present grammatical concepts in the context of effective writing through the use of mentor texts. These mentor text examples, which students read from a writer's perspective, deepen students' metacognition of the importance of these concepts and help them see the elements of grammar as tools for strong writing that authors use strategically to make their work as strong as possible. The goal of the book is to provide middle school English teachers with concrete, user-friendly lesson plans that they can easily use to put mentor-text-based grammar instruction into action in their classrooms.

These lesson plans feature published examples of grammatical concepts from contemporary young adult and middle-grade novels, activities that help students connect their reading and writing experiences, and reflective activities designed to facilitate students' metacognition of the importance of grammatical concepts. This book merges research and practice in concrete and direct ways: each lesson plan is based on principles of mentor text-based grammar instruction designed to deepen students' awareness of what grammatical concepts are, why they're important to effective writing, how to use them to maximize the effectiveness of their own works, and how incorporating them can enhance the quality of their own writing. The thorough plans in this book are designed to help you put the best practices of grammar instruction into action in your teaching in concrete, practitioner-oriented ways that are informed by key research findings on the teaching of grammar. The ideas, examples, and instructional suggestions will give you the necessary resources to incorporate mentor-text-based grammar lessons that develop students' metacognition of the tools of effective grammar and communication. Now, let's look even more closely at exactly what to expect in this book by considering its key features and topics.

What to Expect in This Book

This book contains 15 detailed mentor-text-based lesson plans on grammar instruction, each of which will provide you with a clear and informative explanation of its focal grammatical concept, a published mentor text that exemplifies that concept, and instructional steps to use when helping your students understand the features of a grammatical concept, comprehend its importance, and connect it to their writing. For consistency and ease of use, each of the book's lesson plans follows this format:

- Overview: an overarching description of the key features and goals of the lesson.
- Objectives: an identification of key content students will learn.
- Time Frame: the number of class periods the lesson is designed to take. (While this is a recommended time frame, you should certainly feel free to adapt the time spent on the lesson to what you feel would be best for your students.)
- Background Knowledge Required: what students need to know before getting started with the lesson.
- Materials Needed: materials and resources to have on hand for the lesson.
- Detailed Plan: step-by-step directions for conducting the lesson. The detailed lesson plan provides:
  ◊ A potential script to use with your students or adapt as needed. In each plan, the potential script is provided as a series of quotations.
  ◊ Information about the focal concept to share with students during an introductory mini-lesson.
  ◊ One or more graphic organizers that can help students understand the grammatical concept.
  ◊ A published mentor text that exemplifies strong use of the grammatical concept.

- ◇ Ideas about how to conduct all of the lesson's instructional activities with your students.
- ◇ Additional instructional recommendations for delivering the lesson, which are included in italics.
- ◆ Differentiation Suggestions: recommendations for differentiating the lesson for students who need additional support or who have advanced understandings of the content.
- ◆ Assessment: ideas for how to assess students' understandings of the focal concept.
- ◆ Notes: a place to make notes on what worked during the lesson and what you might adapt the next time you teach it.

The 15 lesson plans in this book are divided into three sections: Lesson Plans Recommended for the Sixth-Grade English Classroom, Lesson Plans Recommended for the Seventh-Grade English Classroom, and Lesson Plans Recommended for the Eighth-Grade English Classroom, with five lessons associated with each of these three grade levels. Each lesson represents a specific grammatical concept; I connected the grammatical concepts and grade levels by looking closely at a wide range of state grammar, writing, and language standards as well as the Common Core State Language Standards and using this information to identify grade levels at which certain grammatical concepts are often discussed. However, I encourage you to not feel limited by the grade levels associated with these grammatical concepts. My recommendation is to use all of the lesson plans in this book in the ways that best serve your students. For example, if you teach seventh grade, you might use some of the lessons from the sixth-grade section to ensure that your students have strong understandings of concepts that you feel are especially important, and you might also incorporate some lessons from the eighth-grade section when your students seem ready to learn that information. In addition, you could use these lessons as tools for differentiation with small groups or individual students by providing needed review and extra support with an earlier-grade lesson plan or by using an older-grade lesson plan to provide differentiated learning opportunities for students with advanced knowledge of grammar. There are many ways to flexibly make use of the book's range lesson plans in ways that best meet the needs of your students!

Figure I.1 lists all of the grammatical concepts addressed in this book and the lesson plan in which each concept is addressed.

In addition to these three sections of lesson plans, this book contains a fourth section titled "Final Thoughts and Resources." In this section, you'll first find a concluding chapter titled "Using This Book to Maximize Grammar Instruction," which synthesizes key ideas from the book and shares closing

Grammatical Concepts	Associated Lesson Plans
Pronoun case	Lesson 6.1
Intensive pronouns	Lesson 6.2
Punctuation that sets off additional information	Lesson 6.3
Adjectives	Lesson 6.4
Adverbs	Lesson 6.5
Prepositional phrases	Lesson 7.1
Relative clauses	Lesson 7.2
Strong verbs and specific nouns	Lesson 7.3
Connotation and denotation	Lesson 7.4
Simple sentences, compound, and complex sentences	Lesson 7.5
Active and passive voices	Lesson 8.1
Punctuation that indicates a pause or break	Lesson 8.2
Comparative and superlative degrees	Lesson 8.3
Verbals	Lesson 8.4
The indicative, imperative, interrogative, conditional, and subjunctive verb moods	Lesson 8.5

Figure I.1 Grammatical Concepts and Associated Lesson Plans

suggestions for putting its lessons into practice as effectively as possible. After that, you'll encounter Appendix A: Annotated Bibliography of Mentor Texts, which is designed to provide you with a quick reference guide to all of the mentor text examples used in this book. The annotated bibliography contains the titles and authors of the works of literature featured in this book, a key grammatical concept found in each work, and excerpt from that work, previously featured in one of the book's lesson plans, that demonstrates exactly how the author uses that grammatical concept. This annotated bibliography is available electronically from the Routledge website so that you can have easily accessible electronic copies of these mentor texts. Finally, you'll come to Appendix B: Reproducible Graphic Organizers. This resource contains all of the graphic organizers featured in the book's lesson plans. The graphic organizers are grouped by their corresponding lesson plans for clarity and convenient access. These graphic organizers can be downloaded from the Routledge website to help make the book's resources as easy to use as possible.

I believe that teaching grammar in engaging and meaningful ways that use mentor texts and develop students' metacognitive understandings of grammatical concepts is such an important way to help our students grow as writers, readers, and thinkers. Now that we have explored the best practices of grammar instruction, the ways those practices align with this book's approach, and the book's key features, let's go! Keep reading to begin your exploration of these grammar lesson plans!

References

Anderson, J. (2005). *Mechanically inclined*. Stenhouse.

Cook, L. S. (2020). Students as their own best critics: A metacognitive approach to teaching grammar in context. *ATEG Journal, 29,* 14–25.

Dorfman, L. R., & Cappelli, R. (2007). *Mentor texts: Teaching writing through children's literature, K-6*. Stenhouse.

Flavell, J. H. (1979). Metacognition and cognitive monitoring. *American Psychologist, 34,* 906–911.

Marchetti, A., & O'Dell, R. (2015). *Writing with mentors: How to reach every writer in the room using current, engaging mentor texts*. Heinemann.

National Council of Teachers of English (2016). NCTE professional knowledge for the teaching of writing. Retrieved from https://ncte.org/statement/teaching-writing/

Ruday, S. (2020). *The middle school grammar toolkit: Using mentor texts to teach standards-based language and grammar in grades 6–8*. Routledge Eye on Education.

Smagorinsky, P. (2018). *Teaching English by design: How to create and carry out instructional units*. Heinemann.

Thomas, A. (2023). *Nic Blake and the remarkables: The manifestor prophecy*. Balzer + Bray.

Watson, R. (2019). *Some places more than others*. Bloomsbury Children's Books.

Weaver, C. (1998). Teaching grammar in the context of writing. In C. Weaver (Ed.), *Lessons to share on teaching grammar in context* (pp. 18–38). Boynton/Cook.

Wotjer, S. (1998). Facilitating the use of description—And grammar. In C. Weaver (Ed.), *Lessons to share on teaching grammar in context* (pp. 95–99). Boynton/Cook.

SECTION ONE

Lesson Plans Recommended for the Sixth-Grade English Classroom

Lesson 6.1

The Case of Communication: Pronoun Case

Overview

This lesson focuses on the concept of pronoun case, which consists of the subjective, objective, and possessive cases that pronouns can take. The lesson consists of two class periods. On the first day, students will learn about the subjective, objective, and possessive cases; explore how they are used in published texts; and reflect on their importance to writing. On the second day, students will review the attributes of these pronoun cases, apply them to their writing, and consider how the pronoun case they use in their writing can impact the clarity and effectiveness of their work. Students will then conclude the instructional process by describing how they will use this concept in their future work.

Objectives

- Students will understand the concept of pronoun case and the features of the subjective, objective, and possessive pronoun cases.
- Students will understand the importance of pronoun case to effective writing.
- Students will apply the idea of pronoun case to their writing and reflect on the significance of doing so.

DOI: 10.4324/9781003466826-3

Time Frame

Two class periods

Background Knowledge Required

Students should have a fundamental understanding of the concept of pronouns. Students should also understand the ideas of direct object, indirect object, and object of a preposition—this will provide them with background knowledge that will help them understand the objective pronoun case.

Materials Needed

- Figures 6.1.1–6.1.7. These figures are displayed in the lesson plan. They can also be found in Appendix B: Reproducible Graphic Organizers and on the book's website.
- A board, projector, or piece of chart paper to display information.
- Paper on which students will write.

Detailed Plan

Day One
1. Introduction
Here, you'll introduce students to the idea of pronoun case, present the key questions they'll investigate in their first session on pronoun case, and share the agenda for their work that day.

> Today, we're going to explore a grammatical concept called pronoun case, which is an important part of using pronouns in ways that are clear and easy to understand. These are the key questions we'll examine today:
>
> - What is pronoun case?
> - Why is pronoun case important to effective writing?
>
> Now, let's take a look at today's agenda. These are the activities we'll do that will help us answer our questions on pronoun case:

- ◆ Mini-lesson
- ◆ Mentor text examples
- ◆ Mentor text discussion and analysis activities
- ◆ Exit question

I recommend displaying the key questions and the agenda items while sharing them with students.

2. Mini-Lesson

In this mini-lesson, you'll introduce students to the topic of pronoun case, discuss the three cases that pronouns can take, share with students examples of these cases, describe how they're used, and discuss the importance of each of these cases.

> We're going to begin discussing pronoun case. I'll introduce you to key information, examples, and ideas about this topic. This is the starting point for the work we're going to do on the grammatical concept of pronoun case. We'll first talk about what pronoun case is. When we use a pronoun to take the place of a noun, there are different forms, or cases, that we use. The three pronoun cases are subjective, objective, and possessive. These cases are important because they give the reader information about the role they play in the sentence. If we use one case when we should use another, the reader could be confused. We'll look at each of these three cases individually, starting with the subjective case.
>
> The subjective case is the pronoun that we use when referring to the subject of a statement. For example, let's take the sentence 'Kim is playing in the game.' Kim is the subject of this sentence, so a pronoun used in place of her name would be a subjective case pronoun. If Kim uses the pronouns she/her/hers, we would write a version of this sentence that uses a pronoun in place of Kim's name as 'She is playing in the game.' Subjective case pronouns are important because they show that the nouns they're representing are subjects of a statement. Let's look at a chart that summarizes key information regarding subjective case pronouns.

I recommend displaying this chart, as well as the other charts depicted in this mini-lesson, on a projector screen or recreating it on a piece of chart paper as you discuss it with students.

> Now, let's talk about our next pronoun case: the objective case. We use the objective case when a pronoun takes the place of a noun that

Pronoun Case	How It's Used	Examples	Example Used in a Sentence	Why It's Important
Subjective Case	We use the subjective case when referring to the subject of a statement.	I, We, You, He, She, It, They	**She** is playing in the game.	Subjective case pronouns clearly communicate to readers that they represent the subject of a statement without repeating the noun.

Figure 6.1.1 Subjective Case Pronoun Information

Pronoun Case	How It's Used	Examples	Example Used in a Sentence	Why It's Important
Objective Case	We use the objective case when referring to something that is in the "object" role in a statement, such as a direct object, indirect object, or object of a preposition.	Me, Us, You, Him, Her, It, Them	The dog saw **him**.	Objective case pronouns clearly communicate to readers that they represent a noun that is the "object" of something without repeating the noun.

Figure 6.1.2 Objective Case Pronoun Information

is acting as the 'object' of something in a statement, such as when it functions as a direct object, indirect object, or an object of a preposition. For instance, in the sentence, 'The dog saw Brian,' Brian is the direct object in the sentence, so a pronoun used in place of Brian's name would be an objective case pronoun. If Brian uses the pronouns he/him/his, then a version of this sentence that uses a pronoun in place of 'Brian' would read 'The dog saw him.' Objective case pronouns let readers know that they're standing in for a noun that takes an 'object' role. Now, let's look at a chart that contains information about subjective case pronouns.

The final pronoun case we're going to discuss is the possessive case. We use possessive case pronouns to show possession while taking the place of nouns. For example, let's look at the sentence 'That is Kate's ball.' If Kate uses she/her/hers pronouns, we can use the possessive pronoun 'her' in place of 'Kate's' to show that the ball belongs to Kate. This version of the sentence would read

Pronoun Case	How It's Used	Examples	Examples Used in a Sentence	Why It's Important
Possessive Case	We use possessive case pronouns to show possession while taking the place of nouns.	My, Mine, Our, Ours, Your, Yours, His, Her, Hers, Its, Their, Theirs	That is **her** ball. That is **hers**.	Possessive case pronouns are important because of the ways they help us show possession in a piece of writing without repeating a person's name.

Figure 6.1.3 Possessive Case Pronoun Information

Published Example of Subjective Case	Published Example of Objective Case	Published Example of Possessive Case
"**I** was excited for the start of summer" (Cartaya, 2018, p. 4). From *The Epic Fail of Arturo Zamora* by Pablo Cartaya	"Newcharlie wasn't talking to **me**" (Woodson, 2010, p. 2). From *Miracle's Boys* by Jacqueline Woodson	"Homesickness pinched **my** heart for a moment" (Venkatraman, 2019, p. 22). From *The Bridge Home* by Padma Venkatraman

Figure 6.1.4 Published Examples of Pronoun Cases

'That is her ball.' In this example, the possessive pronoun 'her' takes the place of 'Kate's' and shows possession. Possessive pronouns can also be used in place of both the name of the person possessing the item and the item they possess. For instance, we could also rewrite the sentence 'That is Kate's ball' as 'That is hers.' In this example, 'hers' takes the place of both 'Kate's' and 'ball.' Possessive pronouns are important because of the ways they help us show possession in a piece of writing without repeating a person's name. Let's now check out a chart containing key ideas about possessive case pronouns.

3. Mentor Text Examples

In this part of the lesson, you'll share with students published examples of each of the pronoun cases. Examining published mentor texts such as these provides students with authentic examples of this grammatical concept and prepares them to think further about the significance of this concept later in the lesson.

"I'm going to share with you published examples of each of the pronoun cases we're discussing. In each example, the relevant pronoun is in bold."

I recommend displaying these examples, reading them aloud, identifying the relevant pronoun case example, and explaining to students why that pronoun is an example of its particular case.

4. Mentor Text Discussion and Analysis Activities

In this part of the lesson, you'll lead students through activities designed to help them understand the importance of each pronoun case to the mentor text in which it appears.

> Now that we've looked at mentor text examples of pronoun case, we'll explore why these pronoun case examples are important to the quality of the authors' works. Let's look at each mentor text and reflect on why the pronoun case in that example is important.

I suggest displaying Figure 6.1.5, talking with students about why the subjective case pronoun is important to the effectiveness of the sentence, and recording highlights of the conversation in the right-hand column. During this discussion, you can help students understand that the subjective case pronoun is important because it shows readers that the pronoun refers to the subject of the statement.

Next, I recommend displaying Figure 6.1.6, which applies the same analytical focus to the objective case mentor text. When discussing this example with students, you can help them understand the objective case pronoun "me" shows readers that the person being discussed plays an objective role in the sentence.

To conclude this activity, I recommend displaying Figure 6.1.7, which takes the same discussion and analysis-based approach to the possessive pronoun mentor text. While talking with students about this example, I suggest emphasizing that the

Subjective Case Pronoun Mentor Text	Why the Subjective Case Pronoun Is Important to the Text
"**I** was excited for the start of summer" (Cartaya, 2018, p. 4).	

Figure 6.1.5 Subjective Case Pronoun Mentor Text Discussion Chart

Objective Case Pronoun Mentor Text	Why the Objective Case Pronoun Is Important to the Text
"Newcharlie wasn't talking to **me**" (Woodson, 2010, p. 2).	

Figure 6.1.6 Objective Case Pronoun Mentor Text Discussion Chart

Possessive Case Pronoun Mentor Text	Why the Objective Case Pronoun Is Important to the Text
"Homesickness pinched **my** heart for a moment" (Venkatraman, 2019, p. 22).	

Figure 6.1.7 Possessive Case Pronoun Mentor Text Discussion Chart

possessive pronoun shows that the speaker uses the possessive pronoun "my" to show readers that the object she is describing belongs to her.

5. Exit Question

This class period ends with an exit question that asks students to reflect on a key idea regarding what they learned that day about pronoun case.

"The last activity we'll do today is an exit question. I'll ask you to write a response to a question related to our work today on pronoun case. After you write, I'll ask for two volunteers to share their ideas and then I'll collect everyone's response. The exit question is: 'Why is pronoun case important to clear and effective writing?'"

I recommend displaying this question for students. After students turn in their responses,

I review their work before the next class and use it to inform my instruction, noting any strengths and areas of need.

Day Two
1. Introduction
To begin this second day of instruction, you'll talk with students about how they'll build on their previous work on pronoun case, share with them the key questions on pronoun case they'll explore that day, and discuss the day's agenda.

> Great work yesterday on pronoun case! You learned about the subjective, objective, and pronoun cases, explored mentor text examples of each of these cases, analyzed their importance, and answered an exit question about the importance of pronoun case to effective writing. Today, we're going to build on that work. First, we'll review key points about pronoun case. After that, we'll connect the concept of pronoun case to our writing and reflect on its significance. We'll close with an exit question about using pronoun case in our future writing. Our key questions for today are:
>
> ◆ How can we apply the idea of pronoun case to our writing?
> ◆ Why is pronoun case important to the effectiveness of our writing?
>
> Let's check out the agenda for our work today on pronoun case:
>
> ◆ Pronoun case review
> ◆ Writing activity
> ◆ Reflection
> ◆ Exit question

I like to display this information as I share it with students.

2. Pronoun Case Review
In this instructional step, you'll review the key information you shared in the previous day's introductory mini-lesson about the features and importance of the pronoun cases.

> We're going to begin today's work by reviewing important ideas, information, and examples of the subjective, objective, and possessive pronoun cases. I'm going to share with you the charts we discussed in yesterday's mini-lesson about each of these pronoun cases.

To conduct this review of the pronoun cases, I recommend displaying Figures 6.1.1–6.1.3 and revisiting the features and attributes of the subjective, objective, and possessive cases. This is also an excellent opportunity to discuss anything that might have been confusing or challenging for students in the previous class.

3. Writing Activity

This step of the instructional process asks students to create a sentence about a real or fictional event, use an example of one of the three pronoun cases in their work, and identify the case of that pronoun.

"Now that we've reviewed pronoun case information, we're going to do a writing activity with pronoun case. You'll create a sentence about a real or fictional event. In your sentence, you'll use an example of one of the three pronoun cases—personal, subjective, or possessive—in your sentence, and identify that pronoun's case. Before you get started, I'll share with you an example I created. This example is about my family's dog, Newton: 'I took a long walk around the neighborhood with Newton.' In this sentence, I used the subjective case pronoun 'I.'"

I recommend creating and displaying an example that is meaningful to you and that you feel will engage your students.

"Now I'm going to ask you to create a sentence that uses a subjective, objective, or possessive case pronoun, underline the pronoun you used, and identify its case. Once you've finished, I'll ask you to share with a partner, and we'll take volunteers to share with the class."

While students write, I like to move around the classroom to check in with students and monitor their progress. I use this opportunity to provide any additional support students need as they compose their works and identify the relevant pronoun case.

"Next, please share what you created with your partner. Read the text you created, identify the pronoun, and say what case it is."

During this time, I again recommend circulating the classroom to hear students' insights, praise strong work, and provide any clarification and support.

"Great work sharing those responses. Let's now take two volunteers to share with the class the text they created, the pronoun in it, and the case of that pronoun."

When students do this, I suggest calling attention to strengths of their responses and providing any additional explanation or clarification.

4. Reflection

In this section of the instructional process, students revisit the work they created in the writing activity and reflect on the importance of the pronoun case they used.

Now, I'm going to ask you to reflect on the importance of the pronoun case that you used in the piece of writing you just created. I'll ask you to respond to the question 'Why is the pronoun case that you used important to the text you wrote?'

I recommend posting this question on a slide, the board, or a piece of chart paper.

Before you do this, I'm going to share the response I wrote about the text I created. I created the text 'I took a long walk around the neighborhood with Newton,' which uses the pronoun 'I.' My answer to the response question is 'The subjective case is important because it shows I am the subject of the statement.' If I used a different pronoun case, readers would be confused about who the subject of the statement is.

I recommend modeling this reflection with the example that you shared with your students earlier in the lesson.

Now, it's time for you to do the same thing with your passage. Look back at the text you created and write a response to the question 'Why is the pronoun case that you used important to the text you wrote?'

While the students create these responses, I suggest circulating the classroom, calling attention to strengths of their work, and making any recommendations to help them develop their statements.

"Great job on those reflections. Now, share your response with a partner and listen to what they created."

While students share their responses with partners, I like to again move around the room and listen to their insights.

"Now, let's take two volunteers to share their responses with the whole class. After that, please turn in your reflections and the passages you created in our previous activity."

When students share their work, I like to call attention to the strengths of their statements and build on any responses that can be further developed.

5. Exit Question

To conclude this instructional process, students respond to an exit question about pronoun case.

To conclude our work, please write a response to an exit question on pronoun case. I'll ask for two volunteers to share their responses. I'll then collect what everyone has written. The exit question is 'How will you use the concept of pronoun case in your future writing?'

I recommend displaying this exit question as you read it. When students share their responses, I like to praise especially strong aspects of their work.

Differentiation Suggestions

This lesson can be differentiated in a number of ways:

- Students can work with additional mentor texts that use pronoun case so that they are exposed to more examples of pronoun case use.
- Students can work with published pronoun case mentor texts on a variety of reading levels so that they engage with texts that are good fits for them.
- Students can use multiple pronouns in the passage they create.
    - These pronouns can represent different cases so that they can see how multiple pronoun cases can be used in the same sentence.
- Students can create multiple passages that use different pronoun cases.

Assessment

I recommend assessing students' understandings of pronoun case and their work on this lesson sequence in two ways:

- Students' exit question responses.
    - The exit question responses students create provide useful information about their understandings of pronoun case and the role of this concept in effective writing. When examining students' responses to the day one exit question "Why is pronoun case important to clear and effective writing?," I use their responses to determine their awareness of the features of pronoun case and how writers use it to help others understand the information in their work. When evaluating students' responses to the second day's exit question, "How will you use the concept of pronoun case in your future writing?," I assess students' understandings of how this concept can play a role in their future writing and the reasons they will use it in their work.

- Students' writing activities and corresponding reflections.
  - I also recommend assessing students' knowledge of pronoun case by looking at the writing activities and corresponding reflections they created. I recommend evaluating students' written responses to see if they used one of the pronoun cases you've discussed and if they identified it correctly. Then, I suggest assessing their responses to determine how well they understand the importance of the pronoun case they used to the piece they created.

Notes

- What worked when teaching this lesson?
- What might you adapt or change the next time you teach it?

References

Cartaya, P. (2018). *The epic fail of Arturo Zamora*. Puffin Books.
Venkatraman, P. (2019). *The bridge home*. Puffin Books.
Woodson, J. (2010). *Miracle's boys*. Nancy Paulsen Books.

Lesson 6.2

Bringing the Intensity: Intensive Pronouns

Overview

This lesson focuses on the concept of intensive pronouns, which are used to provide extra emphasis to a statement. The lesson is divided into two class periods. On the first day, students will learn what intensive pronouns are and examine examples of them. After that, they will explore how writers use intensive pronouns and the ways that using them can impact a piece of writing. On the second day, students will review the features and importance of intensive pronouns and then apply this grammatical concept to their writing. After using intensive pronouns in their writing, students will reflect on how doing so affects their work. Students will then reflect on ways they might use intensive pronouns in their future writing and the reasons they would use this grammatical concept. At the conclusion of the instructional sequence, students will share something they learned about the importance of intensive pronouns to effective writing.

Objectives

- Students will understand the features of intensive pronouns.
- Students will understand the importance of intensive pronouns to effective writing.
- Students will be able to apply intensive pronouns to their writing and reflect on the impact of doing so.

Time Frame

Two class periods

Background Knowledge Required

Students should have a fundamental understanding of the concept of pronouns.

Materials Needed

- Figures 6.2.1–6.2.4. These figures are displayed in the lesson plan. They can also be found in Appendix B: Reproducible Graphic Organizers and in electronic format on the book's website.
- A board, projector, or piece of chart paper to display information.
- Paper on which students will write.

Detailed Plan

Day One
1. Introduction

To begin this instructional process, you'll introduce students to the focal topic of intensive pronouns, share with them the key questions they'll examine in their first day of work on this topic, and provide them with the agenda for the day's work.

> Today, we're going to learn about a type of pronoun that can make writing especially powerful and intense. They're called intensive pronouns, and they live up to their name! We're going to explore these key questions in our work today:
>
> - What are intensive pronouns?
> - Why are intensive pronouns important to effective writing?
>
> I'm going to share with you our agenda for the day. These activities will help us answer our key questions on intensive pronouns:
>
> - Mini-lesson
> - Mentor text example

- Mentor text discussion and analysis activities
- Exit question

I recommend displaying the key questions and the agenda items on a slide or on the board while sharing them with students.

2. Mini-Lesson

You'll conduct a mini-lesson on key features of intensive pronouns. This mini-lesson is designed to introduce students to what intensive pronouns are, what they look like, and why they're used.

> I'm going to introduce you to some key information about intensive pronouns. This will be a starting point for the rest of the work we do on this topic. We'll continue to talk about this information as we discuss intensive pronouns in more detail.
>
> First, let's talk about what intensive pronouns are. Intensive pronouns are pronouns that end with 'self' or 'selves' and are used to add extra emphasis to a statement. The words 'himself, herself, myself, yourself, yourselves, itself, themself, themselves,' and 'ourselves' are all intensive pronouns. For example, we might say 'The mayor herself came to visit our school' or 'I met the author himself!' In these sentences, the words 'herself' and 'himself' are intensive pronouns. They add extra emphasis to the information in the sentence and they end with 'self' or 'selves.' If we remove an intensive pronoun from a sentence, that sentence will still make sense, but it won't have the same level of emphasis that it would with an intensive pronoun in it. We use intensive pronouns when we want to really emphasize

Grammatical Concept	What Are Intensive Pronouns?	What Are Examples of Intensive Pronouns?	How Can Intensive Pronouns Look in Writing?	Why Are Intensive Pronouns Important?
Intensive pronouns	Intensive pronouns are pronouns that end with 'self' or 'selves' and are used to add extra emphasis to a statement.	The words himself, herself, myself, yourself, yourselves, itself, themself, themselves, and ourselves are all intensive pronouns.	The mayor **herself** came to visit our school. I met the author **himself**!	Intensive pronouns are important to effective writing because they are a way for writers to add extra emphasis to a statement.

Figure 6.2.1 Intensive Pronoun Information

something. They are a tool that writers use to give that extra 'oomph' to their statements!

Let's take a look at an informational chart on intensive pronouns. It highlights and summarizes key ideas about this grammatical concept.

I recommend displaying this chart as you discuss it with students.

"Now that we've looked at this information about intensive pronouns, let's explore how they can appear in a published text!"

3. Mentor Text Example

In this step of the lesson, you'll share with students a published mentor text that contains intensive pronouns. This provides students with an authentic example of how intensive pronouns are used and prepares them to think further about the significance of this concept later in the lesson.

Take a look at this passage from the book *Omar Rising* by Aisha Saeed (2022): 'When I was accepted to Ghalib, the headmaster had called me himself to tell me the news' (p. 211). In this passage, author Aisha Saeed, through the narration of Omar, the book's protagonist, uses the intensive pronoun 'himself.' Next, we'll think together about the importance of the intensive pronoun to this passage.

As you share the mentor text example with students, I suggest displaying it on a slide or a piece of chart paper so that students can follow along with and see the text.

4. Mentor Text Discussion and Analysis Activities

This stage of the lesson focuses on leading the students through a discussion of the intensive pronoun mentor text and corresponding activities that help them understand the importance of the intensive pronoun to the mentor text.

In this discussion, we're going to consider why the intensive pronoun 'himself' is important to the passage from *Omar Rising* that we just examined. First, let's compare the original version of the text that contains the intensive pronoun 'himself' with a revised version that does not use this intensive pronoun.

I recommend displaying these examples on a projector screen or recreating them on a slide or piece of chart paper as you discuss them with students.

Now that we've looked at these examples, we're going to do a follow up activity with them. Please talk with a partner about these two

Original Text Containing Intensive Pronoun	Revised Version with Intensive Pronoun Removed
"When I was accepted to Ghalib, the headmaster had called me himself to tell me the news" (Saeed, 2022, p. 211).	When I was accepted to Ghalib, the headmaster had called me to tell me the news.

Figure 6.2.2 Original Text Containing Intensive Pronoun vs. Revised Version with Intensive Pronoun Removed

questions: How is the passage different without the intensive pronoun 'himself?' and Why do you think the author chose to use an intensive pronoun in this sentence? I'm going to display a graphic organizer that lists these questions and has space for responses under the questions. After you talk with your partners, I'm going to ask for volunteers to share their responses to the questions with the whole class.

I suggest displaying this chart on a projector screen or recreating it on a slide or a piece of chart paper. When students share their responses to the questions with the whole class, I recommend highlights of those responses on the graphic organizer.

Reflection Question One	Reflection Question Two
How is the passage different without the intensive pronoun 'himself?'	Why do you think the author chose to use an intensive pronoun in this sentence?

Figure 6.2.3 Intensive Pronoun Reflection Questions Graphic Organizer

5. Exit Question

This class period ends with an exit question, in which students write a response to a question related to what they've learned that day about intensive pronouns.

> For our final activity of the day, I'm going to ask you to write a response to an exit question related to our work today on intensive pronouns. Please write your response on a piece of paper. I'll ask for two volunteers to share their responses verbally and then I'll collect everyone's written responses. Today's exit question is 'Why would a writer use an intensive pronoun in their work?'

I recommend displaying this question as you read it. After students turn in their responses, I review those examples before the next class and use them to inform my instruction, revisiting anything about which students need additional support.

Day Two

1. Introduction

To begin this second day of instruction, you'll talk with students about how what they'll do that day builds on the ideas from the previous class, share with them the key questions that will guide their work that day, and discuss the agenda for the day's work.

> Great job on your recent work on intensive pronouns! You learned what intensive pronouns are, examined a mentor text example from the book *Omar Rising* by Aisha Saeed (2022) that uses an intensive pronoun, analyzed the importance of the intensive pronoun used in the mentor text, and then answered an exit question about why a writer would use an intensive pronoun in their work. In our work today, we're going to take what we did yesterday and build on it: after we review some key information about intensive pronouns, we're going to apply this concept to our own writing and reflect on its importance. We'll then follow that with some more reflection on intensive pronouns by thinking about how we'll use this concept in our future writing and why. Our key questions today are as follows:
>
> ◆ How can we apply intensive pronouns to our writing?
> ◆ How do intensive pronouns make a difference in our writing?
>
> Now, let's take a look at our agenda for today, which outlines our learning activities for the day's work on intensive pronouns:

What Are Intensive Pronouns?	What Are Some Examples of Intensive Pronouns?	Why Are Intensive Pronouns Important?	What Is a Published Example of Intensive Pronoun Use?
Intensive pronouns are pronouns that end with 'self' or 'selves' and are used to add extra emphasis to a statement.	The words himself, herself, myself, yourself, yourselves, itself, themself, themselves, and ourselves are all intensive pronouns.	Intensive pronouns are important to effective writing because they are a way for writers to add extra emphasis to a statement.	"When I was accepted to Ghalib, the headmaster had called me himself to tell me the news" from the book *Omar Rising* (Saeed, 2022, p. 211).

Figure 6.2.4 Intensive Pronouns Review Information

- Intensive pronoun review
- Writing activity
- Reflection
- Exit question

I like to display this information on a slide or on the board as I share it with students.

2. Intensive Pronoun Review

In this part of the instructional process, you'll conduct a brief review of the features, importance, and examples of intensive pronouns discussed in the previous day's lesson.

> Before we get into our writing and reflective activities today, we're going to recap some important ideas and examples related to intensive pronouns, their importance, and their uses. This chart provides key information that will help us review the concept of intensive pronouns.

When sharing this review information with students, I suggest reading the information, explanation, and example out loud with students. In addition, if students' work in the previous class indicated any confusion or misunderstanding about intensive pronouns, this is a good time to discuss anything that you feel would benefit students.

3. Writing Activity

This next step in the instructional process transitions to students applying the concept of intensive pronouns to their writing. It asks students to create a brief passage, true or fictional, that uses an intensive pronoun.

> Now that we've reviewed important information and examples related to intensive pronouns, we're going to do an activity in which you'll

use an intensive pronoun in your writing. I'll ask you to create a short passage of one or two sentences that uses an intensive pronoun to provide extra emphasis to a statement. This can be about a true situation or a fictional one—it's totally up to you!

Before you do this, I'll share with you an example I created: 'Joe went to a Pittsburgh Penguins game and had an amazing time! He saw a great game and met Sidney Crosby <u>himself</u>!' In this sentence, I used the intensive pronoun 'himself' to provide extra emphasis. As you can see, I underlined this word in the passage.

While you can certainly use this example with your students, I recommend creating an example that is meaningful to you and that you feel will resonate with your students and displaying it for them.

Now, I'm going to ask you to create a passage of your own that uses an intensive pronoun to add extra emphasis to a statement. Please underline the intensive pronoun you used like I did in my example. Once you've finished, I'll ask you to share with a partner and then I'll ask for volunteers to share their examples with the class.

As students write, I suggest circulating the classroom to monitor their progress, identify strengths of their work, and clarify any confusion.

"Now that you've created these intensive pronoun examples, please share what you created with a partner. Read to them the text you created and identify the intensive pronoun you used."

While students do this, I recommend again circulating the classroom, this time to listen to what students share with their partners. While you listen to what the students share with their partners, I suggest praising strong work and providing any needed support and clarification.

"Great job sharing those responses with your partners. Now, let's take two volunteers to share with the rest of us the passage you created and identify the intensive pronoun you used."

When students share their work with the large group, I recommend again noting particular strengths of their responses and providing further explanation when relevant.

4. Reflection

This part of the instructional process asks students to return to the written text they just created in the previous writing activity and analyze the importance of the intensive pronoun they used to the piece they created.

In this activity, I'm going to ask you to reflect on the importance of the intensive pronoun you used to the piece of writing that you created. I'm going to ask you to write in response to the question 'Why is the intensive pronoun you used important to the text that you created?'

I recommend posting this question on a slide, the board, or a piece of chart paper.

Before you write your response, I'll share with you the response that I wrote about the text I created. I recently shared the passage 'Joe went to a Pittsburgh Penguins game and had an amazing time! He saw a great game and met Sidney Crosby himself!' with you. Here is my answer to the response question: 'The intensive pronoun himself is important to the text I created because it emphasizes that Joe met Sidney Crosby, who is the captain of the team and an all-time great hockey player. Since meeting a great player like Sidney Crosby can be such a big deal to a hockey fan, I wanted to use an intensive pronoun to emphasize it.'

I recommend modeling this reflection with the example that you shared with your students earlier in the lesson.

"Now, it's your turn. Look back at the text you created in our last activity and write a response to the question 'Why is the intensive pronoun you used important to the text that you created?'"

As students work on these responses, I recommend moving around the room and monitoring their progress. I like to observe what students are writing, calling attention to any strengths that they've exhibited and encouraging them to develop ideas in more detail when relevant

"Great job reflecting on those ideas. Now, share with a partner the response that you created and listen as they share their response with you."

During this time, I suggest again circulating the classroom, praising strong work and asking clarification questions when applicable.

Thanks for sharing those responses with your partners and listening to their insights. Let's take two volunteers to share with the large group your answer to the reflection question. After that, please turn in these reflections as well as the writing activity you completed before it.

As students share these insights, I recommend again calling attention to strong responses and building on any student response that can be enhanced with additional explanation.

5. Exit Question

At this final stage of the instructional process, students respond to an exit question about the importance of intensive pronouns.

"I'm going to ask you to write a response to an exit question on intensive pronouns. After you do so, I'll ask for two volunteers to share their responses verbally, and then I'll collect everyone's written responses. Today's exit question is 'Why are intensive pronouns important tools for effective writing?'"

I suggest displaying this exit question as you read it. When students verbally share their ideas, I like to comment on especially strong components of their responses and elaborate on ideas that can be even further expanded.

Differentiation Suggestions

This lesson can be differentiated in a number of ways:

- Students can work with additional mentor texts that use intensive pronouns so that they are exposed to more examples of this concept in published works.
- Students can work with published intensive pronoun mentor texts on a variety of reading levels so that they engage with texts that are good fits for them.
- Students can use multiple intensive pronouns in the passage they create.
- Students can create multiple passages that use intensive pronouns.

Assessment

I recommend assessing students' understandings of intensive pronouns and their work on this lesson sequence in two ways:

- Students' exit question responses.
    - The exit question responses students create during this instructional sequence provide useful information about their understandings of intensive pronouns and their role in effective writing. When examining students' responses to the day one exit question, "Why would a writer use an intensive pronoun in their work?," I determine their awareness of the fact that writers use intensive pronouns to add emphasis to especially important statements.

Similarly, when evaluating students' responses to the day two exit question, "Why are intensive pronouns important tools for effective writing?," I look to see if students understand the key ideas we've explored throughout the lesson sequence, such as the fact that we can use intensive pronouns strategically to increase the level of emphasis in a piece of writing.
- Students' writing activities and corresponding reflections.
    - I also recommend assessing students' knowledge of intensive pronouns by looking closely at their work from the writing activities and corresponding reflections they created on the second day of the instructional process. I suggest evaluating their written responses to see if they used an intensive pronoun, and if so, if they used it in a way that adds emphasis to the piece they created. When evaluating students' written responses, I recommend assessing the level of understanding they demonstrate of why intensive pronouns are important tools for effective writing and the amount of detail they use when sharing those insights.

Notes

- What worked when teaching this lesson?
- What might you adapt or change the next time you teach it?

Reference

Saeed, A. (2022). *Omar rising*. Nancy Paulsen Books.

Lesson 6.3

Adding and Clarifying: Punctuation that Sets Off Additional Information

Overview

This lesson focuses on how writers can use punctuation, such as commas, parentheses, or dashes, to set off or separate additional information from the rest of the sentence. The lesson spans two class periods. On the first day, students will learn what it means to use punctuation to set off or separate additional information in a sentence, exploring how and why writers do this. On the second day, students will review this concept, apply it to their own writing, and reflect on how using punctuation to set off additional information is important to the effectiveness of their works. At the conclusion of the instructional process, students will consider how this concept can be important to their future writing.

Objectives

- Students will understand what it means to use punctuation to set off or separate additional information from the rest of a sentence.
- Students will know punctuation marks they can use to set off additional information.
- Students will be able to use punctuation to set off additional information in their own writing and reflect on the importance of this concept.

DOI: 10.4324/9781003466826-5

Time Frame

Two class periods.

Background Knowledge Required

Students should be familiar with commas, parentheses, and dashes so that they will be able to understand the lesson content when those punctuation marks are discussed.

Materials Needed

- Figures 6.3.1 through 6.3.5. These figures are displayed in the lesson plan. They can also be found in Appendix B: Reproducible Graphic Organizers and in electronic format on the book's website.
- A board, projector, or piece of chart paper to display information.
- Paper on which students will write.

Detailed Plan

Day One
1. Introduction
To begin this instructional process, you'll introduce students to the topic of using punctuation to set off additional information in a sentence, share the key questions they'll investigate in their first day working on this topic, and present the agenda for the day.

> Today, we're going to explore an important grammatical concept—punctuation that writers use to set off or separate additional information in a sentence. We'll examine these questions:
>
> - What does it mean to use punctuation to set off additional information in a sentence?
> - What punctuation marks do writers use to do this?
> - Why is doing this important to effective writing?
>
> Let's take a look at the agenda for our work today:
>
> - Mini-lesson
> - Mentor text examples

36 ♦ Adding and Clarifying: Punctuation that Sets Off Additional Information

- ♦ Mentor text discussion and analysis activities
- ♦ Exit question

I suggest displaying the key questions and the agenda items while talking with students about them.

2. Mini-Lesson

At this stage of the instructional process, you'll conduct a mini-lesson on the concept of using punctuation to set off additional information. In this mini-lesson, you'll introduce students to the topic, identify punctuation that can be used for this purpose, and discuss why using punctuation in this way is important.

> In this mini-lesson, we'll begin to think about using punctuation to set off additional information from the rest of a sentence. We'll discuss what this concept is, examine examples of punctuation that can set off additional information, and talk about why it is important. This is the first step in our work together on this topic. You don't need to memorize this information now—we'll continue to discuss these ideas together as we work on this topic.
>
> First, let's talk about what it means to use punctuation to set off additional information. When we write, we sometimes provide our readers with additional information that is not essential to the sentence's meaning and is separate from the main part of the sentence. To show our readers that this information is extra and not part of the main sentence, we separate that information from the main part of the sentence using punctuation. There are three forms of punctuation

Grammatical Concept	What Is It?	What Are Some Examples Used in Sentences?	What Is It Important?
Punctuation That Sets Off Additional Information	Punctuation, such as commas, parentheses, and dashes, that is used to separate additional information from the main part of a sentence.	Newton, my amazing dog, greeted me at the door. Newton (my amazing dog) greeted me at the door. Newton—my amazing dog—greeted me at the door.	This concept is important because it identifies extra information for the reader.

Figure 6.3.1 Information about Punctuation That Sets Off Additional Information

that are frequently used to separate additional information from the main part of the sentence—commas, parentheses, and dashes. Writers can use any of these kinds of punctuation to set off additional information.

Using punctuation to separate additional information from the main part of the sentence is important because it shows the reader that the information is extra and is not needed for the sentence to make sense. It's like a signal for the reader that says 'This is extra information.' Let's take a look at a chart that highlights and summarizes key information on this topic.

I recommend displaying this chart on a projector screen or recreating it on a piece of chart paper as you discuss it with students.

"Now, let's check out how punctuation that sets off additional information can appear in published texts!"

3. Mentor Text Examples

In this activity, you'll share with students published examples of punctuation that sets off additional information. By exploring published mentor texts such as these, students will see authentic examples of this grammatical concept and be prepared to reflect later in the lesson on the importance of this concept.

"Let's look together at published examples of punctuation that sets off additional information. I'm going to share with you three published sentences—each one uses punctuation to set off additional information. As you'll see, one sentence uses commas for this purpose, one uses parentheses, and one uses dashes."

I suggest displaying these examples and reading them aloud. As you read them, I recommend pointing out the punctuation in each example that sets off additional information and the information set off by that punctuation.

Published Example Using Commas	**Published Examples Using Parentheses**	**Published Example Using Dashes**
"It was a mystery in itself, whatever it was, and Lina was determined to solve it" (DuPrau, 2003, p. 96). From *The City of Ember* by Jeanne DuPrau	"The rumors about me have gone from fantastical (Godzilla with a crew cut) to realistic (assistant principal)" (Cartaya, 2019, p. 2). From *Marcus Vega Doesn't Speak Spanish* by Pablo Cartaya	"He says he's too full for dessert, and–as casually as possible–excuses himself from the dinner table" (Hiaasen, 2023, p. 183). From *Wrecker* by Carl Hiaasen

Figure 6.3.2 Published Examples of Punctuation That Sets Off Additional Information

4. Mentor Text Discussion and Analysis Activities

This part of the lesson focuses on helping students think about the importance of the punctuation used in the mentor text examples to set off additional information. The discussion and activities described here are designed to develop students' understandings of the significance of this use of punctuation.

> Now that we've looked at these examples of punctuation that sets off additional information, we'll explore why this punctuation is important to these texts. We'll compare each original published example with a new version that does not contain punctuation that sets off additional information and discuss the importance of that punctuation.

I recommend displaying Figure 6.3.3, talking with students about why the commas that separate text from the rest of the sentence are important, and recording highlights from the conversation in the right-hand column. During this discussion, you can help students understand that these commas are important because they let readers know that the statement "whatever it was" provides additional information not essential to the sentence's meaning.

Next, I suggest displaying Figure 6.3.4, discussing with students the importance of the parentheses used in the original sentence, and writing key points in the right-column. In this conversation, I recommend helping students understand that

Mentor Text Example	Example Without Commas That Set Off Additional Information	Why the Commas Are Important to the Text
"It was a mystery in itself, whatever it was, and Lina was determined to solve it" (DuPrau, 2003, p. 96).	It was a mystery in itself whatever it was and Lina was determined to solve it.	

Figure 6.3.3 Mentor Text Discussion Chart: Commas That Set Off Additional Information

Mentor Text Example	Example Without Parentheses That Set Off Additional Information	Why the Parentheses Are Important to the Text
"The rumors about me have gone from fantastical (Godzilla with a crew cut) to realistic (assistant principal)" (Cartaya, 2019, p. 2).	The rumors about me have gone from fantastical Godzilla with a crew cut to realistic assistant principal.	

Figure 6.3.4 Mentor Text Discussion Chart: Parentheses That Set Off Additional Information

Mentor Text Example	Example Without Dashes That Set Off Additional Information	Why the Dashes Are Important to the Text
"He says he's too full for dessert, and–as casually as possible–excuses himself from the dinner table" (Hiaasen, 2023, p. 183).	He says he's too full for dessert, and as casually as possible excuses himself from the dinner table.	

Figure 6.3.5 Mentor Text Discussion Chart: Dashes That Set Off Additional Information

the parentheses are important because they clearly show the reader that the statements "Godzilla with a crew cut" and "assistant principal" are extra details.

I recommend concluding this mentor text activity by displaying Figure 6.3.5, conducting a discussion with students about the importance of the dashes in the sentence, and noting important insights in the right-hand column. During the discussion, I suggest helping students think about how these dashes are important because they show that "as casually as possible" is extra information in the sentence.

5. Exit Question

This session concludes with an exit question in which students reflect on key information they learned that day about punctuation that sets off additional information.

> We'll conclude today's work with an exit question. To answer this question, you'll write a response to a question about our work today. I'll ask for two volunteers to share; after that, I'll collect everyone's answers. The exit question is 'Why do writers use punctuation to set off additional information?'

I suggest displaying this question while students write their answers. I recommend using the students' responses to inform future instruction, addressing any areas of confusion.

Day Two
1. Introduction

To introduce this second day of instruction on punctuation that sets off additional information, you'll tell students how they'll build on their previous work on this topic, present the day's focal questions, and share the agenda.

> Yesterday, we worked hard on punctuation! We talked about punctuation that sets off additional information, exploring what it is,

examining examples, and discussing why this concept is important to effective writing. Today, we'll build on yesterday's work. We'll start by reviewing information about this topic, and then we'll connect this grammatical concept to our own writing. After that, we'll reflect on the significance of using this kind of punctuation in our works. We'll finish with an exit question about how we'll use punctuation that sets off additional information in the writing we'll do in the future. The questions we'll explore today are:

- How can we use punctuation that sets off additional information in our writing?
- Why is using punctuation that sets off additional information important to the quality of our writing?

Here is today's agenda:

- Review of punctuation that sets off additional information
- Writing application
- Reflection
- Exit question

I recommend displaying this information while sharing it.

2. Review of Punctuation that Sets Off Additional Information

In this stage of the instructional process, you'll review the information you shared in the previous day's opening mini-lesson about features, examples, and importance of punctuation that sets off additional information.

We'll get started by reviewing key information about punctuation that sets off additional information in a sentence. I'm going to share with you the chart we looked at in yesterday's mini-lesson that discusses what this concept is, provides examples of it, and describes its importance.

To review this information about punctuation that sets off additional information, I suggest displaying Figure 6.3.1 and going over the description, features, examples, and importance of punctuation that sets off additional information. I also recommend using this time to further discuss any aspects of this concept about which students have questions or have shown any confusion.

3. Writing Activity

In this step of the instructional process, students will create a sentence that uses punctuation to set off additional information. They will choose whether to use commas, parentheses, or dashes for this purpose.

> Now, we're going to use our knowledge of punctuation that sets off additional information in a writing activity. You'll create a sentence about a topic of your choice, and you'll use punctuation to set off additional information from the rest of the sentence. You can use any of the punctuation types we've discussed today—commas, parentheses, or dashes—to set off that information. Before you start, I'll share an example I created: 'Autumn—my favorite season—brings cool air and colorful leaves to my town.' In this sentence, I used dashes to set off the additional information of 'my favorite season,' but I could have used either parentheses or commas instead.

I suggest creating and displaying an example that is relevant to you and that you feel will be engaging to your students.

"It's your turn. Create a sentence that uses commas, parentheses, or dashes to set off additional information. Once you're done, I'll ask you to share your example with a partner. You'll read your example to them, tell them which punctuation you used to set off additional information, and identify that additional information."

While students work, I recommend moving around the classroom, checking on their progress, and providing any additional support they need.

"Now that you've finished creating those examples, share what you created with a partner. Remember to tell them the punctuation you used to set off additional information and the additional information you included."

As students share with partners, I like to again circulate the room to hear what they share, praise strong work, and provide support when helpful.

"Excellent job sharing that information with a partner. Now, let's take two volunteers to share what they created with the rest of the class."

When student volunteers share, I call attention to strong aspects of their work and provide any clarification or further explanation that might be helpful.

4. Reflection

During this activity, students look closely at the work they created in the writing activity and reflect on the importance of the punctuation they used to set off additional information.

In this next activity, I'm going to ask you to return to the piece of writing you just created and reflect on the importance of the punctuation that you used to set off additional information in that passage. I'll ask you to write a response to the question 'Why is the punctuation that sets off additional information important to the passage you created?'

I like to post this question in front of the class while sharing it with students.

"Before you answer, I'll share my response about the passage I wrote. My passage was 'Autumn—my favorite season—brings cool air and colorful leaves to my town.' My answer to the response question was 'The dashes I used to set off additional information are important because they show that 'my favorite season' is extra detail that I added to the sentence. If I didn't use punctuation to set off this information, readers might not know that this is extra detail I added that is separate from the rest of the sentence.'"

I suggest modeling this reflection with the example you created and shared with your students.

"It's your turn. Return to what you wrote and compose a response to the question 'Why is the punctuation that sets off additional information important to the passage you created?'"

As students write their responses, I recommend checking in on them to monitor their progress. This is a great opportunity to provide students with individualized support.

"Now, share your response with a partner and listen to their insights."

As students share with their partners, I like to again circulate the classroom and hear their ideas.

"We'll now take two volunteers to share their ideas verbally. After that, everyone will turn in their reflections and the passages they created in the writing activity."

When students share their responses, I recommend calling attention to especially strong points and building on any statements that can be enhanced with further information.

5. Exit Question

At the conclusion of the instructional process, students answer an exit question about punctuation that sets off additional information.

We'll wrap up our work with an exit question on punctuation that sets off additional information. After you write a response to the exit question, two volunteers will share their responses, and then I'll collect what everyone has written. The exit question is 'How can using punctuation to set off additional information be important to your future writing?'

I like to display the exit question as I read it. After students share their responses, I recommend praising especially strong points they make.

Differentiation Suggestions

This lesson can be differentiated in a number of ways:

- Students can explore additional mentor text examples that use punctuation to set off additional information at various locations in sentences, such as the beginnings, middles, and endings of sentences, so that they can further see the different, flexible ways this concept can be used.
- Students can examine mentor examples of this concept on a range of reading levels so that they can work with texts that fit well with them.
- Students can create multiple passages in the writing activity. Each of these passages can include a different type of punctuation that sets off additional information.
- Students can create a single passage that uses punctuation to set off additional information multiple times.

Assessment

I suggest assessing students' understandings of punctuation that sets off additional information and their work on this instructional process in two ways:

- Students' exit question responses:
  - Students' responses to the two exit questions in this lesson sequence provide important information about their understanding of punctuation that sets off additional information and the role of this concept in strong writing. When considering students' responses to the day one exit question "Why do writers use punctuation to set off additional information?," I use their answers to gauge their understandings of what this concept is and the way it

can make writing clear for the reader. When examining students' responses to the day two exit question "How can using punctuation to set off additional information be important to your future writing?," I evaluate students' awareness of how they can incorporate this concept in their writing and the impact that this writing tool can have on their work.

- Students' writing activities and corresponding reflections:
  - I also suggest evaluating students' understandings of punctuation that sets off additional information by assessing the writing activities and corresponding reflections they created. When looking at their written responses, I recommend determining if students used punctuation to set off additional information, if the information they set off was in fact additional information, and if they used the punctuation marks correctly. When assessing students' written responses, I recommend evaluating how well they understand why the punctuation they used to set off additional information is important to the reader's ability to understand the passage.

Notes

- What worked when teaching this lesson?
- What might you adapt or change the next time you teach it?

References

Cartaya, P. (2019). *Marcus Vega doesn't speak Spanish.* Penguin Random House.
DuPrau, J. (2003). *The city of Ember.* Yearling.
Hiaasen, C. (2023). *Wrecker.* Alfred A. Knopf.

Lesson 6.4

Developing and Describing: Adjectives

Overview

This lesson addresses the concept of adjectives—descriptive words that provide information about a noun or pronoun. The lesson spans two class periods. On the first day, students will learn about the features of adjectives, look at examples of them, explore how writers use them, and consider their impact on writing. The next day, students will review the concept of adjectives, apply it to their own writing, and reflect on how this concept impacts the effectiveness of their works. To conclude the process, students will answer an exit question about why adjectives are important tools for effective writing.

Objectives

- Students will understand the concept of adjectives.
- Students will understand the importance of adjectives to effective writing.
- Students will be able to use adjectives in their own writing and reflect on the importance of doing so.

DOI: 10.4324/9781003466826-6

Time Frame

Two class periods.

Background Knowledge Required

Students will need to know the concepts of nouns and pronouns to understand what adjectives describe.

Materials Needed

- Figures 6.4.1–6.4.4. These figures are displayed in the lesson plan. They can also be found in Appendix B: Reproducible Graphic Organizers and in electronic format on the book's website.
- A board, projector, or piece of chart paper to display information.
- Paper on which students will write.

Detailed Plan

Day One

1. Introduction

To introduce this instructional process, you'll first let students know that they'll be studying the concept of adjectives. After that, you'll present the key questions the class will explore in the first session on adjectives and then share the agenda for the day.

> We're going to examine the grammatical concept of adjectives, which are descriptive words that provide information about a noun or pronoun. We'll consider these questions in class today:
>
> - What are adjectives?
> - Why are adjectives important to effective writing?
>
> Let's now check out today's agenda. These activities will help us answer our questions on adjectives:
>
> - Mini-lesson
> - Mentor text example

- Mentor text discussion and analysis activities
- Exit question

I suggest displaying the day's questions and agenda items while presenting them to students.

2. Mini-Lesson

Here, you'll teach a mini-lesson on key features of adjectives. In it, you'll introduce students to what adjectives are, provide them with some examples, and discuss their importance.

> In this mini-lesson, I'll share some important information on adjectives. This is the starting point for the work we'll do together on this topic. You don't need to memorize this information now—we'll continue to discuss these ideas in more detail as we talk about adjectives.
>
> Let's first talk about what adjectives are. Adjectives are words that provide descriptive information about a noun or pronoun. For example, in the sentence 'Look at this beautiful dog!,' the word 'beautiful' is an adjective. It provides descriptive information about the dog. Similarly, in the sentence 'I read a unique book,' 'unique' is an adjective. This word describes the book. Another example is in the sentence 'We saw the huge building.' 'Huge' is an adjective that describes the building. All of these words provide descriptive information that helps the reader understand the characteristics of the noun being described. Since adjectives can enhance the reader's knowledge of the noun or pronoun they're describing, they're important tools for effective writing. I'm going to share with you an informational chart on adjectives.

Grammatical Concept	What Are Adjectives?	What Are Some Examples of Adjectives?	What Are Some Ways Adjectives Can Look in Writing?	Why Are Adjectives Important?
Adjectives	Adjectives are descriptive words that provide information about a noun or pronoun.	Some examples of adjectives are young, old, warm, frigid, green, beautiful, unique, huge, majestic, fast, and enjoyable.	We saw the **majestic** lion. The **fast** player sprinted down the field. They enjoyed the **warm** day.	Adjectives are important to effective writing because they help the reader understand the characteristics of the noun or pronoun being described.

Figure 6.4.1 Adjective Information

It highlights key information about what adjectives are, what they look like, how they're used, and why they're important.

I suggest projecting this chart on a screen or recreating it on a large piece of paper while talking with students about this information.

"Let's now deepen our knowledge of adjectives by looking at a published example."

3. Mentor Text Example

Here, you'll share with students a published passage in which an author uses adjectives to provide descriptive information. By doing so, you'll show students how adjectives are used in authentic situations and prepare them for other work they'll do on this concept later in the lesson.

We'll look together at a published example of adjective use from the book *Amina's Voice* by Hena Khan: 'Her green eyes and tiny nose remind me of my next-door neighbor's bad-tempered cat, Smokey' (2018, p. 4). In this passage, author Hena Khan uses several adjectives to add descriptive information: 'green,' 'tiny,' 'next-door,' and 'bad-tempered' are all adjectives used in this sentence. In our next activity, we'll think together about the importance of these adjectives to the passage.

When you share this adjective mentor text example with students, I recommend displaying it on a slide or a piece of chart paper so that students can read along with you.

4. Mentor Text Discussion and Analysis Activities

In this stage of the lesson, you'll lead students through a discussion about the adjective mentor text and related activities designed to help them understand the importance of adjectives to this text. The goal of this work is to facilitate students' awareness of the role of adjectives in writing.

"Now, we're going to think together about why the adjectives are important to the mentor text example from *Amina's Voice* that we examined. Let's compare the original text with a revised version without the adjectives we identified."

Original Text Containing Adjectives	Revised Version with Adjectives Removed
"Her green eyes and tiny nose remind me of my next-door neighbor's bad-tempered cat, Smokey" (Khan, 2018, p. 4).	Her eyes and nose remind me of my neighbor's cat, Smokey.

Figure 6.4.2 Original Text Containing Adjectives vs. Revised Version with Adjectives Removed

Reflection Question One	Reflection Question Two
How is the sentence different without the adjectives?	Why do you think the author used the adjectives in the sentence?

Figure 6.4.3 Adjective Reflection Questions Graphic Organizer

I suggest projecting these examples to the front of the classroom or recreating them on a piece of chart while sharing them with students.

For the next step of this activity, please talk with a partner about these two questions: How is the sentence different without the adjectives? and Why do you think the author used the adjectives in the sentence? After you talk with your partners, I'll ask for volunteers to share their responses with the class. We'll record responses on a graphic organizer that I'll display.

I recommend projecting this chart to the front of the room or recreating it on a piece of chart paper and then recording students' responses on the chart when they share their ideas.

5. Exit Question

At the conclusion of this class period, students answer an exit question related to the importance of adjectives.

"The last thing we'll do today on adjectives is an exit question related to the work we did in class on this concept. Please write your response on a piece of paper. After you write, I'll ask for two volunteers to share, and I'll collect everyone's answers. The exit question is 'Why would a writer use adjectives in their work?'"

I suggest displaying this question as you read it and students write their answers. Once students submit their responses, I examine the answers to evaluate students' understandings. I use this information to inform my upcoming instruction on the topic.

Day Two
1. Introduction
To open the second day of this work on adjectives, you'll discuss how the work students will do that day builds on the previous day's discussion and activities, provide the day's focal questions, and share the agenda for the second day of work on this topic.

> Excellent job yesterday working on adjectives! In yesterday's class, we discussed what adjectives are and why they're important. After that, we looked at a passage from the book *Amina's Voice* (Khan, 2018) that is a great adjective mentor text. We then reflected on the impact the adjectives had on the passage before closing with an exit question about why writers use adjectives. Today, we'll build on that work and go into even more depth with adjectives. First, we'll review important ideas about adjectives. Then we'll apply this concept to our own writing and think about its significance. Afterwards, we'll consider why adjectives are important tools for effective writing. Here are our key questions for today:
>
> ◆ How can we use adjectives in our writing?
> ◆ How can adjectives impact the description and detail in our writing?
>
> Our agenda for today is as follows:
>
> ◆ Adjective review
> ◆ Writing activity using adjectives
> ◆ Reflection
> ◆ Exit question

I like to display the key questions and agenda items while sharing them with students.

2. Review of Adjectives
Here, you'll review for students key ideas, examples, and explanations about adjectives you shared and discussed in the previous day's work.

"Let's recap some key information about adjectives that we discussed yesterday. We'll look together at a chart that reviews what adjectives are, some examples of them, why they're important, and how they can be used."

What Are Adjectives?	What Are Some Examples of Adjectives?	Why Are Adjectives Important?	What Is a Published Example of Adjective Use?
Adjectives are descriptive words that provide information about a noun or pronoun.	Some examples of adjectives are young, old, warm, frigid, green, beautiful, unique, huge, majestic, fast, and enjoyable.	Adjectives are important to effective writing because they help the reader understand the characteristics of the noun or pronoun being described.	"Her **green** eyes and **tiny** nose remind me of my **next-door** neighbor's **bad-tempered** cat, Smokey" (Khan, 2018, p. 4).

Figure 6.4.4 Adjective Review Information

I recommend displaying this chart and reading the information on it out loud while students follow along. This is also a great time to further discuss any aspects of adjective use that may have been confusing to students in the previous day's class.

3. Writing Activity

In this activity, students apply the concept of adjectives to their writing. They create a brief passage that uses an adjective to provide descriptive information about a noun or pronoun.

> We're going to take what we've learned about adjectives and put it into action in our own writing! You'll create a one or two-sentence passage that uses an adjective to describe a noun or pronoun in a piece of writing. You can write about any topic you want—the only requirement is to use an adjective in your work!
>
> Before you start, I'll share an example I created: 'I rested my head on the <u>soft</u> pillow.' In this sentence, I used the adjective 'soft' to provide descriptive information. I underlined that adjective in the text.

I suggest creating an example of your own that uses an adjective to provide description, sharing it with your students, and displaying it for them.

> Now, it's your turn! You'll create a passage that uses an adjective to provide description, and you'll underline the adjective in your passage like I did in the example. Afterwards, I'll ask you to share your example with a partner. Volunteers will share with the rest of the class.

While students work on these examples, I suggest moving around the classroom and monitoring their progress. This is a great time to provide support and praise strong work.

"Good job working on these examples. Next, share with a partner the passage you created and identify the adjective you used."

During this time, I recommend circulating and listening to what students share. This is another excellent opportunity to support students and praise excellent work.

"Let's have two volunteers share with the class the passage you created, identifying the adjective you used in it."

While students share these ideas with the class, I like to again praise strong work and provide any relevant explanation and information.

4. Reflection

In this reflective activity, students return to the passage they created in the previous writing activity and analyze the importance of the adjective they used to the piece they wrote.

> We're going to move to a new activity. In it, you'll reflect on the importance of the adjective that you used to the passage you just wrote. You'll write a response to the question 'Why is the adjective you used important to the text you created?'

I suggest posting this question while sharing it with students.

> Before you do this, I'll share the reflection I wrote about my passage, which was 'I rested my head on the soft pillow.' My answer to the reflection question is 'The adjective soft is important to my sentence because of the description it provides. By using this adjective, I give the reader information about the pillow and let them know that the pillow was soft. Without the adjective, the reader wouldn't have this information.'

I suggest modeling this reflection with the adjective example that you shared with your students, discussing why the adjective you used is important to the passage you shared.

"It's your turn now. Revisit the passage you created that uses an adjective and write an answer to the question 'Why is the adjective you used important to the text you created?'"

While students compose these responses, I recommend circulating the classroom to monitor their progress. During this time, you can provide students with individualized support and praise.

"Good work writing those responses. Please share with a partner the reflection you created and listen as they share theirs."

I like to again move around the classroom while students share these reflections with their peers, listening to their insights and supporting their work.

"Let's take two volunteers to share their answers to the reflection question with the class. After that, I'll ask for all of you to turn in these reflections and the passages you created in our writing activity."

When students share their answers, I suggest again calling attention to particularly strong reflections and building on any statements that can be further developed.

5. Exit Question

This instructional process closes with students responding to an exit question on the importance of adjectives.

We'll conclude this work with an exit question on adjectives. You'll write an answer to an exit question on adjectives and then I'll ask for volunteers to share their responses verbally. After that, I'll collect all of the written responses. The exit question is 'Why are adjectives important tools for effective writing?'

I suggest displaying the exit question while reading it. When students share their responses, I like to commend especially strong insights and comment further on statements that can benefit from additional explanation.

Differentiation Suggestions

This lesson can be differentiated in a number of ways:

- Students can work with additional adjective mentor texts so they encounter additional examples of adjectives in published writing.
- Students can work with published adjective examples on a range of reading levels to help them find texts that best fit with them.
- Students can use multiple adjectives in the passages they create.
- Students can create multiple passages that use adjectives.

Assessment

I recommend assessing students' knowledge of adjectives and their work on this instructional sequence in two ways:

- Students' exit question responses.
  - The two exit question responses students compose and submit during this instructional process provide important information

about their understanding of the concept of adjectives and the role of this concept in effective writing. When evaluating students' responses to the day one exit question "Why would a writer use adjectives in their work?," I suggest assessing how well students explain that writers would use adjectives to add descriptive information to their writing. On a related note, when examining students' responses to the day two exit question "Why are adjectives important tools for effective writing?," I recommend assessing if students are able to explain that adjectives are important because the information in them helps the reader understand the characteristics of the noun or pronoun they are describing.
- Students' writing activities and corresponding reflections.
  - I suggest also assessing students' knowledge of adjectives and their importance by reading their work from the writing activity and corresponding reflection they did on the second day of the instructional process. To assess students' work from the writing activity, I look to see if students used an adjective in their passage, if this adjective adds descriptive information, and if the descriptive information it provides aligns with the passage. When evaluating students' reflections, I assess the detail and insight in their statements about why the adjective they used is important to the text they created.

Notes

- What worked when teaching this lesson?
- What might you adapt or change the next time you teach it?

Reference

Khan, H. (2018). *Amina's voice.* Simon and Schuster.

Lesson 6.5

Explanation and Impact: Adverbs

Overview

This lesson focuses on the concept of adverbs, which are words that describe verbs, adjectives, and other adverbs, answering questions such as "How?," "When?," "Where?," and "To what extent?" The lesson consists of two class periods. During the first day of this instructional sequence, students will learn about key features of adverbs, examine examples of them, look at how writers use them, and think about the impact of adverbs on writing. On the second day, students will review information about adverbs, apply the concept to their writing, and reflect on how adverb use affects their works. At the end of the process, students will respond to an exit question that asks them to consider the importance of adverbs to effective writing.

Objectives

- Students will understand the concept of adverbs.
- Students will understand the importance of adverbs to effective writing.
- Students will be able to use adverbs in their own writing and reflect on the importance of doing so.

Time Frame

Two class periods.

Background Knowledge Required

Students will need to understand the concepts of verbs and adjectives when learning about the kinds of words adverbs can describe.

Materials Needed

- Figures 6.5.1–6.5.4. These figures are depicted in the lesson plan. In addition, they are available in Appendix B: Reproducible Graphic Organizers and electronically on the book's website.
- A board, projector, or piece of chart paper to display information.
- Paper for student writing.

Detailed Plan

Day One
1. Introduction
When introducing this instructional process, you'll begin by letting students know that they'll be learning about adverbs. Next, you'll share the questions that the class will explore in the first season on this topic. Afterward, you'll present the agenda for the day.

> Today, we're going to begin to explore the grammatical concept of adverbs, which are words that describe verbs, adjectives, and other adverbs, answering questions such as 'How?,' 'When?,' 'Where?,' and 'To what extent?' We'll examine these questions today:
>
> - What are adverbs?
> - Why are adverbs important tools for effective writing?
>
> Now, let's look at today's agenda, which lists the activities we'll do in class today as we think about our key questions:

- Mini-lesson
- Mentor text example
- Mentor text discussion and analysis activities
- Exit question

I like to display the key questions and agenda items for the day while sharing them with students.

2. Mini-Lesson

At this point in the instructional sequence, you'll teach a mini-lesson on key components of adverbs. You'll do this by providing introductory information about what adverbs are, sharing examples of them, and discussing the importance of adverbs.

> Now, let's get into our mini-lesson on adverbs. In it, I'll introduce you to key information on adverbs, which will be the foundation for our work on this concept. You don't need to memorize these ideas now—we'll talk about them in more detail as we keep working with adverbs.
>
> We'll start by discussing what adverbs are. Adverbs are words that describe verbs, adjectives, and other adverbs, answering questions such as 'How?,' 'When?,' 'Where?,' and 'To what extent?' Many adverbs end with the letters -ly, but there are also adverbs that don't end this way. Let's look at an example of adverb use. In the sentence 'Julie ran quickly,' 'quickly' is an adverb. It describes how Julie ran

Grammatical Concept	What Are Adverbs?	What Are Some Examples of Adverbs?	What Are Some Ways Adverbs Can Look in Writing?	Why Are Adverbs Important?
Adverbs	Adverbs are words that describe verbs, adjectives, and other adverbs, answering questions such as "How?," "When?," "Where?," and "To what extent?"	Some examples of words that can function as adverbs are quickly, slowly, skillfully, carefully, extremely, soon, often, frequently, immediately, happily, everywhere, exactly, truly, very, and sincerely.	The player **skillfully** kicked the ball. They spoke truly and sincerely. He looked everywhere. We **soon** learned the information. The team played **very** well.	Adverbs are important tools for effective writing because the explanation they provide can enhance a reader's understanding of the piece.

Figure 6.5.1 Adverb Information

and gives an explanation about what is happening in the sentence. Adverbs are important tools for effective writing because the explanation they provide can enhance a reader's understanding of the piece. I'm going to share a chart that contains key information about adverbs. It discusses what adverbs are, identifies examples of them, shows how they can be used in writing, and describes their importance.

I recommend displaying this chart or recreating it on chart paper when sharing the information on it with students.
"Next, we'll examine a published example of adverb use."

3. Mentor Text Example
In this activity, you'll provide students with a published passage in which the author uses an adverb to provide explanation and information. This shows students an authentic example of adverb use and prepares them for other work they'll do with adverbs.

Let's look at a sentence from the book *The Stars Beneath Our Feet* by David Barclay Moore (2017) that uses an adverb: 'As I flew back home, I suddenly realized how heavy the gifts were that I had just brought in that shop' (p. 4). In this excerpt, author David Barclay Moore uses the adverb 'suddenly' to add information and explanation. Next, we'll think further about the significance of this adverb to the text.

When sharing this adverb mentor text with students, I suggest displaying it on a slide or on chart paper.

4. Mentor Text Discussion and Analysis Activities
During this part of the instructional process, you'll discuss the adverb mentor text with students and lead them through activities constructed to help them consider the significance of the adverb to the passage. The discussion and corresponding activities are designed to develop students' awareness of the importance of adverbs to writing.

Let's work together to consider why the adverb 'suddenly' is important to the mentor text we read from *The Stars Beneath Our Feet*. We'll start by comparing the original example with a version that does not contain the adverb 'suddenly.'

I recommend displaying these examples on a projector screen or piece of chart paper while reading them aloud to students.

Original Text Containing an Adverb	Revised Version with Adverb Removed
"As I flew back home, I suddenly realized how heavy the gifts were that I had just bought in that shop" (Moore, 2017, p. 4).	As I flew back home, I realized how heavy the gifts were that I had just bought in that shop.

Figure 6.5.2 Original Text Containing an Adverb vs. Version with Adverb Removed

Reflection Question One	Reflection Question Two
How is the sentence different without the adverb "suddenly"?	Why do you think the author used this adverb in the sentence?

Figure 6.5.3 Adverb Reflection Questions Graphic Organizer

Now, I'm going to ask you to talk with a partner about two questions related to these sentences: How is the sentence different without the adverb 'suddenly'? and Why do you think the author used this adverb in the sentence? After you and your partner discuss these questions, volunteers will share their responses with the class. I'll write your answers on a graphic organizer.

To conduct this activity, I suggest projecting this chart or recreating it on a large piece of paper and recording students' responses on it.

5. Exit Question
This class session closes with students answering an exit question on the significance of adverbs.

For our final activity today, you'll answer an exit question about adverbs. You'll write your response to the question on a piece of paper. I'll ask for two volunteers to share their answers and then I'll collect everyone's work. The exit question is 'Why would writers use adverbs in their writing?'

I recommend displaying this question while reading it to students. After students write their answers and submit their responses, I review them, evaluate the students' understandings, and use their knowledge to inform future instruction.

Day Two
1. Introduction
To begin this second day of work on adverbs, you'll talk with students about how the day's activities build on what they did the day before, share the focal questions, and discuss the agenda for the class period.

> Great work yesterday on adverbs! In yesterday's class, you learned key information about adverbs, looked closely at an adverb mentor text from the book *The Stars Beneath Our Feet* by David Barclay Moore (2017), reflected on the importance of the adverb to the mentor text, and answered an exit question about why writers would use adverbs in their work. Today, we're going to build on yesterday's work. We'll start with a review of information about adverbs. After that, we'll apply adverbs to our writing and think about their importance. We'll close by considering the significance of adverbs to effective writing. Our key questions for today are:
>
> ◆ How can we use adverbs in our work?
> ◆ How do adverbs provide explanation and information in our writing?
>
> Here is our agenda for the day:
>
> ◆ Adverb review
> ◆ Adverb-focused writing activity
> ◆ Reflection
> ◆ Exit question

I suggest projecting these questions and agenda items to the front of the room or writing them on the board while sharing them with students.

2. Adverb Review
At this point in the lesson, you'll review key adverb ideas, examples, and explanations discussed the previous day.

What Are Adverbs?	What Are Some Examples of Adverbs?	Why Are Adverbs Important?	What Is a Published Example of Adverb Use?
Adverbs are words that describe verbs, adjectives, and other adverbs, answering questions such as "How?," "When?," "Where?," and "To what extent?"	Some examples of words that can function as adverbs are quickly, slowly, skillfully, carefully, extremely, soon, often, frequently, immediately, happily, everywhere, exactly, truly, very, and sincerely.	Adverbs are important tools for effective writing because the explanation they provide can enhance a reader's understanding of the piece.	"As I flew back home, I **suddenly** realized how heavy the gifts were that I had just brought in that shop" (Moore, 2017, p. 4).

Figure 6.5.4 Adverb Review Information

Our first agenda item is an adverb review. We'll recap important information about adverbs that we explored yesterday. Let's look at a chart that reviews what adverbs are, provides examples of them, discusses their importance, and shares a published example.

I suggest projecting this chart to the front of the classroom and reading its contents out loud while students read along. If students demonstrated any confusion regarding adverbs in the previous class, I recommend using this review time to discuss any topics that may have been challenging.

3. Writing Activity

In this activity, students apply the concept of adverbs to their writing. They write a brief passage that uses an adverb to provide information and explanation.

We'll now take our work with adverbs to the next level by using them in our writing! You'll create a passage of one or two sentences that uses an adverb to provide information and explanation. Like we've talked about, the explanations that adverbs provide can enhance a reader's understanding of the piece. You can write about any topic—the only requirement is to use an adverb!

Before you write, I'll show you an example I created of a passage containing an adverb: 'The performers danced gracefully across the stage.' I used the adverb 'gracefully' in the sentence to explain how the performers danced and underlined that adverb in the text.

I recommend creating your own sentence that uses an adverb to provide information and explanation, sharing it with your students, and displaying it.

> Now, you'll create a passage of one or two sentences that uses an adverb that can enhance the reader's understanding, and you'll underline the adverb you used like I did. Then, you'll share your examples with a partner; volunteers will share with the class after that.

As students create their passages, I recommend circulating the classroom and checking on how they're doing. I like to use this time to provide needed support and praise strong work.

> "Great work creating those passages. Next, turn to your partner, share the passage you created, and identify the adverb you used in it."

When students share this information, I suggest moving around the classroom, listening to their examples and the adverbs in them, and providing students with additional support and praise.

> "Next, I'll ask for two volunteers to share the passage you created and point out the adverb you used."

As students share their passages and point out their adverbs, I suggest again calling attention to any especially strong examples and providing any needed clarification and support.

4. Reflection

During this step of the instructional process, students revisit the passage they wrote in the preceding activity and reflect on the significance of the adverb they used to that passage.

> In this activity, you'll return to the passage you just created and reflect on the significance of the adverb you used to the passage. You'll write a response to the question 'Why is the adverb you used important to the passage you created?'

I recommend displaying this question while sharing it with students.

> Before you write your reflection, I'll share the one that I wrote about my passage, 'The performers danced gracefully across the stage.' I answered the reflection question by saying 'Gracefully (the adverb I used in my passage) is important to the passage because it tells how the performers danced. This adverb provides an explanation that helps the reader understand exactly how they danced. Without the adverb gracefully, it wouldn't be clear to readers that the performers danced that way.'

I recommend sharing with students your reflection on the adverb example you wrote. This provides students with a model that can inform their reflections.

"Now, it's time for you to write your reflections. Reread the passage you created that uses an adverb and write a response to the question 'Why is the adverb you used important to the passage you created?'"

While students write their responses, I like to move around the classroom to check on how they're doing, provide individualized support, and praise strong work.

"Thanks for your hard work writing those reflections. Now, share what you created with a partner and then they'll share their work with you."

I suggest circulating the classroom while students share with each other. This is another great opportunity to monitor their progress and provide individualized feedback.

"Now, I'll ask for two volunteers to share their reflections out loud. Then, everyone will turn in their reflections and the pieces they wrote in the writing activity."

I recommend praising particularly strong responses that volunteers share and providing any needed explanation or clarification regarding students' statements.

5. Exit Question

To close this instructional process, students respond to an exit question on the importance of adverbs.

> We'll wrap up our work on adverbs with an exit question. You'll write a response to an exit question on adverbs and after that volunteers will share their responses out loud. Then, I'll collect all of the written answers. The exit question is 'Why are adverbs important tools for effective writing?'

I recommend displaying this question and reading it out loud for students. As students share answers, I suggest praising the strengths of excellent responses and elaborating on those that can be further enhanced.

Differentiation Suggestions

This lesson can be differentiated in a variety of ways:

- ◆ Students can explore additional adverb mentor texts, which provides them with increased exposure to adverbs in published works.
- ◆ Students can read adverb mentor texts on a range of reading levels so they can find texts that are well-aligned for them.
- ◆ Students can use multiple adverbs in the passages they create.
- ◆ Students can create multiple passages that feature adverbs in them.

Assessment

I suggest assessing students' knowledge of adverbs and the work they do in this instructional process in two ways:

- Students' exit question responses.
    - The two exit question responses students turn in during this lesson sequence provide important insights regarding their understanding of adverbs and the role that adverbs play in writing. When assessing students' answers to the first-day exit question "Why would writers use adverbs in their writing?," I recommend evaluating how effectively students describe that writers use adverbs to provide explanation and information in their work. Similarly, when assessing students' responses to the second-day exit question "Why are adverbs important tools for effective writing?," I suggest evaluating if students are able to discuss that adverbs are important because the explanation they provide can enhance the reader's understanding of the piece.
- Student's writing activities and corresponding reflections.
    - I also recommend evaluating students' knowledge of adverbs and the importance of this concept to effective writing by examining the passages they created on the second day of the instructional process and their corresponding reflections. When evaluating students' work on the writing activity, I check if students used an adverb in the passage they created, consider the explanation and information the adverb provided, and determine if that explanation and information made sense for the piece. When assessing students' reflections, I look at the amount of detail and the level of insight in their statements about why the adverb is important to the text they created.

Notes

- What worked when teaching this lesson?
- What might you adapt or change the next time you teach it?

Reference

Moore, D. B. (2017). *The stars beneath our feet*. Knopf Books for Young Readers.

SECTION TWO

Lesson Plans Recommended for the Seventh-Grade English Classroom

Lesson 7.1

Developing Ideas: Prepositional Phrases

Overview

This lesson addresses the grammatical concept of prepositional phrases, which are descriptive phrases that begin with a preposition and end with a noun or pronoun that is the object of the preposition. It consists of two class periods. On the first day, students will learn about key aspects of prepositional phrases, look at examples of them, explore how writers use this concept, and consider how prepositional phrases can impact a piece of writing. On the second day, students will review important information about prepositional phrases, apply this concept to their own writing, and reflect on the impact of this concept to the passages they created. The instructional sequence concludes with an exit question that asks students to comment on the importance of prepositional phrases to writing.

Objectives

- Students will understand the concept of prepositional phrases.
- Students will learn the importance of prepositional phrases to effective writing.
- Students will use prepositional phrases in their writing and reflect on the significance of this practice.

DOI: 10.4324/9781003466826-9

Time Frame

Two class periods.

Background Knowledge Required

No specific background knowledge is required. Students will learn about the features and uses of prepositions and prepositional phrases in the lesson.

Materials Needed

- Figures 7.1.1–7.1.5. These figures are displayed in the lesson plan, in Appendix B: Reproducible Graphic Organizers, and in electronic format on the book's website.
- A board, projector, or piece of chart paper to display information.
- Paper for students to use in writing activities.

Detailed Plan

Day One
1. Introduction
To open this instructional sequence, you'll introduce students to the topic of prepositional phrases, present the key questions they'll explore in their first day on this concept, and share the agenda for the day's work.

> We're going to start exploring the concept of prepositional phrases, which are phrases that provide description and detail to a piece of writing. We'll consider these key questions in today's work:
>
> - What are prepositional phrases?
> - Why are prepositional phrases important to effective writing?
>
> Here's our agenda for the day; these activities will help us answer our key questions on prepositional phrases:
>
> - Mini-lesson
> - Mentor text example

- Mentor text discussion and analysis activities
- Exit question

I suggest displaying the day's key questions and agenda while sharing them with students.

2. Mini-Lesson

Here, you'll conduct a mini-lesson on key components of prepositional phrases. In this mini-lesson, you'll discuss the features of prepositional phrases, share examples of them, and describe the importance of prepositional phrases to effective writing.

> In this mini-lesson, I'll introduce you to some key information about prepositional phrases. We'll continue to refer back to these ideas throughout our work on this topic. First, let's discuss the concept of prepositions. Prepositions are words that show relationships between information, like where something is, where an action took place, or when it happened. These words begin prepositional phrases. Prepositional phrases are descriptive phrases that begin with a preposition and end with a noun or pronoun called the object of the preposition. For example, in the sentence 'The players ran on the field,' the word 'on' is a preposition and 'field' is the object of a preposition. The prepositional phrase is 'on the field.' Let's look together at some examples of some frequently used prepositions.

I suggest displaying these preposition examples while you share them with your students.

> Now that we've looked at these preposition examples, let's think further about prepositional phrases. Another prepositional phrase example is found in the sentence 'We ate before the game.' In this sentence, 'before the game' is a prepositional phrase—it begins with the preposition 'before' and ends with 'game,' which is the object of

At	During
Above	In
Across	On
Before	Through
Down	Under

Figure 7.1.1 Some High-Frequency-Prepositions

Grammatical Concept	What Are Prepositional Phrases?	What Are Examples of Prepositional Phrases?	How Can Prepositional Phrases Look in Writing?	Why Are Prepositional Phrases Important?
Prepositional phrases	Prepositional phrases are descriptive phrases that begin with a preposition and end with a noun or pronoun called the object of the preposition.	On the field Before the game Above the clouds During the party	The players ran **on the field**. We ate before the game. The plane flew above the clouds. **During the party**, we celebrated.	Prepositional phrases are important because of the detail and description they add to a statement. This information can enhance the reader's understanding.

Figure 7.1.2 Prepositional Phrase Information

the preposition. Prepositional phrases, like the ones I've shared with you so far and the others we'll think about, are important because of the detail and description they can add to a statement. This information can enhance the reader's understanding. Let's look at a chart on prepositional phrases that highlights key ideas about this concept.

I recommend displaying this chart on a projector screen or recreating it on a piece of chart paper as you talk about its contents.

"Now that we've explored key information about prepositional phrases, let's see how they look in published writing!"

3. Mentor Text Example

During this part of the instructional process, you'll share with students an example of a prepositional phrase from a published text. By examining a published example, students will see how prepositional phrases can appear in authentic situations.

> Take a look at this excerpt from the novel *King and the Dragonflies* by Kacen Callender (2020) that uses a prepositional phrase: 'Cicadas make their noise, and the breeze whispers through the trees' (p. 153). In this sentence, Kacen Callender, the book's author, uses the prepositional phrase 'through the trees' to provide description. In our next activity, we'll think together about why this prepositional phrase is important to the passage.

I recommend displaying this prepositional phrase mentor text and reading it out loud while students follow along.

Original Text Containing Prepositional Phrase	Revised Version without Prepositional Phrase
"Cicadas make their noise, and the breeze whispers through the trees" (Callender, 2020, p. 153).	Cicadas make their noise, and the breeze whispers.

Figure 7.1.3 Original Text vs. Revised Version without Prepositional Phrase

4. Mentor Text Discussion and Analysis Activities

At this point in the lesson, you'll talk with students about the prepositional phrase mentor text and engage them in related activities that help them think about the importance of the prepositional phrase to the published passage. The goal of this work is to develop students' awareness of the impact that prepositional phrases can have on writing.

> Now that we've checked out a prepositional phrase mentor text, we'll think about the importance of the prepositional phrase to the published passage. To get started, let's compare the original text from *King and the Dragonflies* with a revised version without the prepositional phrase 'through the trees.'

I suggest reading these examples out loud to students while displaying them on a projector screen or piece of chart paper.

> Now that we've looked at both of these examples, please talk with a partner about these two questions: How is the sentence different without the prepositional phrase 'through the trees'? and Why do you think the author used this prepositional phrase? Once you talk with your partners, I'll ask for volunteers to share their ideas with the whole class. I'll write responses on a graphic organizer.

I suggest projecting this graphic organizer to the front of the classroom or recreating it where it can be easily seen and writing students' responses in the columns.

5. Exit Question

At the conclusion of this class period, students answer an exit question—a closing question related to what they learned that day about prepositional phrases.

> To close our work for today, you'll respond to an exit question about prepositional phrases. Please write your answer to the question on a piece of paper. I'll ask for two volunteers to share their

Reflection Question One	Reflection Question Two
How is the sentence different without the prepositional phrase "through the trees"?	Why do you think the author used this prepositional phrase?

Figure 7.1.4 Prepositional Phrase Reflection Questions Graphic Organizer

responses out loud before I collect everyone's written answers. The exit question is 'Why would a writer use prepositional phrases in their writing?'

I suggest displaying this question in a visible location while you read it. I recommend reviewing students' written responses to assess their knowledge of the concept and then using their understandings to inform your future instruction.

Day Two
1. Introduction
To open this second day on prepositional phrases, you'll discuss with students how the work they'll do that day builds on the previous day's activities, present the key questions that will guide the lesson, and share the day's agenda.

> Excellent job working on prepositional phrases yesterday! You learned important information about this concept, looked at an example of prepositional phrase use in the book *King and the Dragonflies* by Kacen Callender (2020), considered the significance of the prepositional phrase to that example, and responded to an exit question about why writers would use prepositional phrases. Today,

we'll explore prepositional phrases even further. First, we'll review key ideas about this concept. Then, we'll use prepositional phrases in our writing and reflect on their impact. Finally, we'll answer an exit question about the importance of prepositional phrases to writing. Here are our key questions for today:

- How can we use prepositional phrases in our writing?
- How does using prepositional phrases impact our writing?

Let's now check out our agenda for today, which identifies our activities on prepositional phrases:

- Prepositional phrase review
- Writing activity
- Reflection
- Exit question

I suggest displaying the key questions and agenda items while sharing them with students.

2. Prepositional Phrase Review

In this section of the lesson, you'll briefly review the features, importance, and examples of prepositional phrases discussed the previous day.

Let's review important information about prepositional phrases. We'll look together at a chart that highlights what prepositional phrases are, shares examples, describes their importance, and includes the published example we discussed in our last class.

What Are Prepositional Phrases?	What Are Some Examples of Prepositional Phrases?	Why Are Prepositional Phrases Important?	What Is a Published Example of Prepositional Phrase Use?
Prepositional phrases are descriptive phrases that begin with a preposition and end with a noun or pronoun called the object of the preposition.	On the field Before the game Above the clouds During the party	Prepositional phrases are important because of the detail and description they add to a statement. This information can enhance the reader's understanding.	"Cicadas make their noise, and the breeze whispers **through the trees**" (Callender, 2020, p. 153).

Figure 7.1.5 Prepositional Phrase Review Information

I recommend displaying this chart and reading its contents out loud while students follow along. This is also a great time to review any misunderstandings or confusion students demonstrated in the previous lesson.

3. Writing Activity
This activity calls for students to apply prepositional phrases to their writing. To do so, they compose a passage that uses a prepositional phrase to provide description and detail.

> Let's take the next step in our work with prepositional phrases by applying this concept to our writing! Your job will be to write a one or two sentence that uses a prepositional phrase to add detail and description to the piece and enhances the reader's understanding of information in the passage.
>
> First, I'll share an example of a passage I created that uses a prepositional phrase: 'The runners sprinted <u>up the hill</u>.' I used the prepositional phrase 'up the hill' to provide detail and description regarding where the runners sprinted and underlined it in the passage.

I suggest composing your own sentence that uses a prepositional phrase to add description and detail to a piece, displaying it, and sharing it with your students.

> You'll now create a passage of your own of one or two sentences that uses a prepositional phrase to incorporate detail and description that develops the reader's understanding. Please underline the prepositional phrase you use. Afterwards, you'll share your work with a partner; I'll ask for volunteers to share with the class.

While students write their passages, I suggest moving around the classroom and monitoring their progress.

"Good job using prepositional phrases in your writing. Please turn to a partner, read the passage you created, and identify the prepositional phrase you used."

As students share their work, I recommend circulating the classroom again. This time, you'll listen to students' examples containing prepositional phrases and comment on their work.

"Now, let's have two volunteers share the piece you created and identify the prepositional phrase in it."

When students share their work and identify the prepositional phrases they used, I like to call attention to particularly well-used prepositional phrases and provide any relevant support.

4. Reflection

This part of the lesson builds on the previous activity: students look back at the passage they created and reflect on the importance of the prepositional phrase they used.

> Now, we're going to do a reflective activity. You'll revisit the passage you just created and reflect on the importance of the prepositional phrase you used. You'll write an answer to the question 'Why is the prepositional phrase you used important to the passage you created?'

I like to display this question while reading it out loud.

> First, I'll share the reflection I wrote about my passage, 'The runners sprinted up the hill.' I wrote, 'The prepositional phrase up the hill is important to my passage because it describes the difficulty of what the runners were doing. Since sprinting up a hill is difficult, the prepositional phrase helps the reader understand how hard the runners were working.'

I suggest sharing your reflection about the prepositional phrase example you created, highlighting what information the prepositional phrase adds to the passage.

"You'll now write your reflections. Reread the passage you wrote and write a response to the question 'Why is the prepositional phrase you used important to the passage you created?'"

As students create their responses, I circulate the classroom to see how they're doing with the reflection question, providing support if students need it.

"Good job writing those reflections! Now, share your reflection with a partner and they'll share theirs with you."

I like to move around the room and listen to what students share with each other, offering personalized feedback on their responses.

"Let's have two volunteers share their reflections verbally. Then, I'll ask everyone to turn in their reflections along with the passages you wrote in our last activity."

When volunteers share, I like to praise especially strong insights and provide any further explanation or additional information when needed.

5. Exit Question

This instructional sequence concludes with students answering an exit question on the importance of prepositional phrases.

> We'll close our work on prepositional phrases with an exit question. Everyone will write a response to an exit question, volunteers will

share their answers verbally, and I'll collect everyone's written work. The exit question is 'Why are prepositional phrases important tools for effective writing?'

I recommend displaying this exit question while reading it aloud. When students verbally share answers, I suggest calling attention to particularly insightful points and elaborating on any statements that can be developed even more.

Differentiation Suggestions

There are a number of ways to differentiate this lesson:

- Students can explore additional mentor texts that feature prepositional phrases; this gives them additional exposure to published examples of prepositional phrases.
- Students can read prepositional phrase mentor texts on a range of reading levels so they can work with texts that are good fits for them.
- Students can incorporate multiple prepositional phrases in the passages they write.
- Students can write multiple passages that use prepositional phrases.
- Students can begin prepositional phrases with a variety of prepositions.

Assessment

I like to assess students' knowledge of prepositional phrases and their work in this lesson sequence in two ways:

- Students' exit question responses.
  ◊ Students' answers to the two exit questions in this instructional process provide key information regarding their awareness of prepositional phrases and their role in effective writing. When evaluating students' responses to the day-one exit question "Why would a writer use prepositional phrases in their writing?," I assess how thoroughly and accurately they discuss that writers would use prepositional phrases to add detail and description to a statement. When assessing students' response to the day-two exit question "Why are prepositional phrases important tools

for effective writing?," I evaluate if students can explain that the detail and description prepositional phrases provide can enhance the reader's understanding of a piece.
- ◆ Students' writing activities and corresponding reflections.
  - ◊ I also suggest assessing students' knowledge of prepositional phrases and their importance to strong writing by looking closely at the passages they created and their corresponding reflections. To assess students' work on the passages they created, I determine students used a prepositional phrase, what information that prepositional phrase provided, and if that information aligns with and enhances the piece. When evaluating students' reflections, I look at how thoroughly and insightfully they describe what information the prepositional phrase provides and how this information helps the reader understand the passage.

Notes

- ◆ What worked when teaching this lesson?
- ◆ What might you adapt or change the next time you teach it?

Reference

Callender, K. (2020). *King and the dragonflies*. Scholastic Press.

Lesson 7.2

A Descriptive Tool: Relative Clauses

Overview

This lesson focuses on the concept of relative clauses, which are grammatical tools that describe nouns and pronouns and begin with relative pronouns or relative adverbs. The instructional sequence spans two class periods. During the first day, students will learn the key components of relative clauses, look at examples of them, examine how writers use relative clauses, and think about the impact of this concept. The next day, students will review key information about relative clauses, use this concept in their writing, and reflect on the impact of relative clauses on the pieces they wrote. This instructional process ends with an exit question that asks students to share their thoughts on the importance of relative clauses to writing.

Objectives

- Students will understand what relative clauses are.
- Students will learn the importance of relative clauses to descriptive writing.
- Students will use relative clauses in their writing and reflect on the significance of doing so.

Time Frame

Two class periods.

Background Knowledge Required

Students will need to know the concepts of nouns and pronouns to understand what relative clauses describe.

Materials Needed

- Figures 7.2.1–7.2.5. These figures are displayed in the lesson plan. They are also available in Appendix B: Reproducible Graphic Organizers and on the book's website.
- A board, projector, or piece of chart paper for displaying information.
- Paper for students' writing activities.

Detailed Plan

Day One
1. Introduction
You'll begin this instructional sequence by introducing students to the concept of relative clauses, presenting the key questions students will explore during their first day of work on this topic, and sharing the agenda for the day's class.

Let's begin our exploration of relative clauses! Relative clauses describe nouns and pronouns and begin with relative pronouns or relative adverbs. They're great ways to add description. The big questions we'll consider today are:

- What are relative clauses?
- Why are relative clauses important to writing?

Here's the agenda for today's work. These activities will help us answer our big questions on relative clauses:

- Mini-lesson
- Mentor text example
- Mentor text discussion and analysis activities
- Exit question

I like displaying the day's big questions and agenda items while sharing them with students.

2. Mini-Lesson

After introducing the lesson, you'll conduct a mini-lesson of key aspects of relative clauses. You'll discuss key features of relative clauses, provide examples of them, and describe their importance to effective writing.

> Let's get into our mini-lesson on relative clauses! I'll introduce you to key information on this grammatical concept. This mini-lesson will be a starting point for the rest of the work we do on relative clauses as we continue to work with this concept.
>
> We'll start by talking about what relative clauses are. Relative clauses are descriptive tools that provide information about nouns and pronouns. They begin with relative pronouns or relative adverbs. Let's look at what relative pronouns and relative adverbs are.

I recommend displaying this chart while sharing this information about relative pronouns and relative adverbs with students.

> These relative pronouns and relative adverbs can begin relative clauses by introducing the descriptive information that relative clauses provide. For example, the relative pronoun 'who' could begin the relative clause 'who is a great soccer player.' We could use that relative clause in a sentence by saying 'Sam, who is a great soccer player, is playing today.' Similarly, we could use the relative adverb 'when' to begin the relative clause 'when the soccer game starts.' If we used that relative clause in a sentence, we could say 'I'm excited for 4:00pm, when the soccer game starts.' These relative clauses provide information about the nouns they are describing. Let's look at a chart on relative clauses that includes important information about this concept.

Relative Pronouns	Relative Adverbs
Who, Whose, Whom, Which, That	Where, When, Why

Figure 7.2.1 Relative Pronouns and Relative Adverbs

Grammatical Concept	What Are Relative Clauses?	What Are Examples of Relative Clauses?	How Can Relative Clauses Look in Writing?	Why Are Relative Clauses Important?
Relative clauses	Relative clauses are grammatical concepts that describe nouns and pronouns and begin with relative pronouns or relative adverbs.	who is a great soccer player when the soccer game starts which is her favorite food	Sam, **who is a great soccer player**, is playing today. I'm excited for 4:00pm, **when the soccer game starts.** After the game, Sam will eat pizza, **which is her favorite food.**	Relative clauses are important because they add descriptive information to a piece of writing. The description they provide can enhance the reader's understanding of the noun or pronoun being discussed.

Figure 7.2.2 Relative Clause Information

I suggest displaying this information about relative clauses or recreating it on a piece of chart paper and you discuss it with students.

"Now that we've thought about key information about relative clauses, let's see how they're used in published writing!"

3. Mentor Text Example

In this component of the lesson, you'll share with students a published example of a relative clause. This activity will help students see how relative clauses are used in writing.

> Let's look at an excerpt from the book *The Crossover* by Kwame Alexander (2014) that uses a relative clause: 'He has one pair of Air Jordan sneakers for every month of the year including Air Jordan 1 Low Barack Obama Limited Editions, which he never wears' (p. 11). In this sentence, author Kwame Alexander, through the narration of protagonist Josh Bell, describes Josh's brother's sneaker collection. Alexander uses the relative clause 'which he never wears' to provide description. Next, we'll think together about why this relative clause is important to the sentence.

I recommend displaying this relative clause mentor text and reading it aloud for students.

4. Mentor Text Discussion and Analysis Activities

In this part of the lesson, you'll lead students through a discussion of the relative clause mentor text and corresponding activities to help them consider the importance of the relative clause to that text. This section of the instructional

82 ◆ A Descriptive Tool: Relative Clauses

Original Text Containing Relative Clause	**Revised Version Without Relative Clause**
"He has one pair of Air Jordan sneakers for every month of the year including Air Jordan 1 Low Barack Obama Limited Editions, which he never wears" (Alexander, 2014, p. 11).	He has one pair of Air Jordan sneakers for every month of the year including Air Jordan 1 Low Barack Obama Limited Editions.

Figure 7.2.3 Original Text vs. Revised Version Without Relative Clause

Reflection Question One	**Reflection Question Two**
How is the sentence different without the relative clause "which he never wears"?	Why do you think the author used this relative clause?

Figure 7.2.4 Relative Clause Reflection Questions Graphic Organizer

process is designed to develop students' awareness of why writers use relative clauses.

> In this activity, we'll consider the significance of the relative clause to the mentor text we examined. First, we'll compare the original text from *The Crossover* with a revised version that does not contain the relative clause 'which he never wears.'
>
> *I recommend displaying these examples on a projector screen or piece of chart paper while reading them aloud.*
>
> Please now talk with a partner about these two questions: How is the sentence different without the relative clause 'which he never wears?' and Why do you think the author used this relative clause? I'll display a graphic organizer containing these questions and spaces

underneath them for responses. After you and your partner talk, I'll ask for volunteers to share their ideas with the class. I'll then record responses on the graphic organizer.

I recommend displaying this graphic organizer or recreating it in an easy-to-see location. As students share, I like recording their ideas in the columns.

5. Exit Question
This day of instruction concludes with students answering an exit question connected to what they learned about relative clauses.

> For today's concluding activity, you'll answer an exit question about relative clauses. Please write an answer to the exit question on a piece of paper. I'll ask for two volunteers to share their answers out loud. Then, I'll collect all of the written answers. The exit question is 'Why would a writer use relative clauses in their work?'

I recommend displaying this question while reading it aloud. After collecting students' written answers, I suggest reviewing them to assess students' knowledge and using their understandings to inform upcoming instruction.

Day Two
1. Introduction
You'll begin the second day working on relative clauses by talking with students about how the work they'll do that day builds on the previous class, discussing the key questions that will guide the day's work, and sharing the class's agenda.

> You did great work yesterday on relative clauses! You learned important information about relative clauses, looked at a published example of this concept from the book *The Crossover* by Kwame Alexander (2014), thought about the importance of the relative clause in that example, and answered an exit question about why writers would use relative clauses. Today, we'll take our learning about relative clauses even further: after we review important information about relative clauses, we'll use them in our writing and reflect on their importance to what we wrote. We'll end by answering an exit question about the importance of relative clauses to writing. Our key questions are:
>
> ◆ How can we use relative clauses in our writing?
> ◆ How do relative clauses impact our writing?

What Are Relative Clauses?	What Are Some Examples of Relative Clauses?	Why Are Relative Clauses Important?	What Is a Published Example of Relative Clause Use?
Relative clauses are grammatical concepts that describe nouns and pronouns and begin with relative pronouns or relative adverbs.	who is a great soccer player when the soccer game starts which is her favorite food	Relative clauses are important because they add descriptive information to a piece of writing. The description they provide can enhance the reader's understanding of the noun or pronoun being discussed.	"He has one pair of Air Jordan sneakers for every month of the year including Air Jordan 1 Low Barack Obama Limited Editions, **which he never wears**" (Alexander, 2014, p. 11).

Figure 7.2.5 Relative Clause Review Information

Let's look at today's agenda, which contains our activities on relative clauses:

- Relative clause review
- Writing activity
- Reflection
- Exit question

I recommend displaying the key questions and agenda items while sharing them with students.

2. *Relative Clause Review*

During this part of the lesson, you'll review the features, importance, and examples of relative clauses discussed in the previous class.

"We'll get into our work today by reviewing key ideas about relative clauses. I'll display a chart that shares information about relative clauses, provides examples, discusses their importance, and identifies the published example we examined last class."

I suggest displaying this chart and reading its contents while students follow along. I also recommend using this time to review any confusion or uncertainties students have about relative clauses.

3. *Writing Activity*

In this writing activity, students apply the concept of relative clauses to their own works by composing a passage that uses a relative clause to describe a noun or pronoun.

For our next activity, we'll use relative clauses in our writing. You'll write a passage of one or two sentences that uses a relative clause that adds descriptive information about a noun or pronoun in the piece and enhances the reader's understanding of that noun or pronoun.

"Before you write, I'll share a passage I created that contains a relative clause: Dave, <u>who is an excellent baker</u>, made us a cake. I used the relative clause 'who is an excellent baker' to describe Dave and underlined it in the text."

I recommend writing a passage that uses a relative clause to provide descriptive information about a noun or pronoun, displaying the text, and reading it aloud.

It's your turn! You'll write a passage of one or two sentences that uses a relative to provide descriptive information about a noun or pronoun in the piece. Please underline the relative clause in your passage. After you finish, you'll share your work with a partner; volunteers will share their work with the class.

As students write, I recommend moving around the room and checking on their progress, praising strong work and providing needed support.

"Great work incorporating relative clauses in your writing. Now, turn to a partner, read your passage, and point out the relative clause you used."

While students do this, I like to again circulate the classroom, listening to their passages and taking note of the relative clauses they used.

"Thanks for sharing your work. Let's have two volunteers share their passages and point out their relative clauses."

When students share their passages and relative clauses, I suggest praising particularly strong relative clause examples and sharing any explanation or clarifications that students need.

4. Reflection

In this step of the instructional process, students revisit the passage they wrote in the previous activity and reflect on the significance of the relative clause they used.

Now, we're going to reflect on the relative clauses we used! You'll revisit the piece you just wrote and reflect on the importance of the relative clause you used. You'll write an answer to the question 'Why is the relative clause you used important to the passage you created?'

I recommend displaying this question while reading it aloud.

Before you write, I'll share the reflection I wrote about the passage 'Dave, who is an excellent baker, made us a cake.' I wrote 'The relative clause who is an excellent baker is important to the passage because it provides descriptive information about Dave that enhances the reader's understanding of the situation. It lets readers know that the cake will likely be good because it's being made by an excellent baker.'

I suggest sharing your reflection about the relative clause you used in your passage, discussing the descriptive information it provides and how that information enhances the reader's understanding.

"It's time for you to write your reflections. Please write a response to the question 'Why is the relative clause you used important to the passage you created?'"

While students write, I move around the classroom to monitor their progress on the reflection, providing needed support.

"Nice job working on your relative clause reflections. Please share your reflection with a partner and they'll do the same with you."

I circulate the classroom again during this time, listening to the reflections students share with partners and commenting when relevant.

"We'll take two volunteers to share their answers to the relative clause reflection question. Afterwards, everyone will turn in their reflections and the passages they created in the writing activity."

I recommend praising especially strong reflections that volunteers share and providing additional explanation or clarification when relevant.

5. Exit Question

To conclude this instructional process, students answer an exit question on the significance of relative clauses.

To conclude our work on relative clauses, I'll ask you to write an answer to an exit question on this concept. After you do so, I'll ask for two volunteers to share their responses verbally, and then I'll collect everyone's written answers. The exit question is 'Why are relative clauses important tools for effective writing?'

I suggest displaying this question while reading it. When volunteers share their answers, I recommend praising especially strong statements and elaborating on ideas that can be further developed.

Differentiation Suggestions

There are a variety of ways to differentiate this lesson:

- Students can examine additional relative clause mentor texts, giving them increased exposure to published relative clause examples.
- Students can read relative clause mentor texts on a range of grade levels, allowing them to engage with texts that are good fits for them.
- Students can use multiple relative clauses in the passages they create.
- Students can write multiple passages that contain relative clauses.
- Students can begin relative clauses with a range of relative pronouns or relative adverbs.

Assessment

I recommend assessing students' knowledge of relative clauses and their work in this instructional process in these ways:

- Students' exit question responses
  - Students' answers to the two exit questions in this lesson sequence offer insight into their understandings of relative clauses. When I assess students' responses to the first-day exit question "Why would a writer use relative clauses in their work?," I evaluate how well the students' responses explain that writers would use relative clauses to describe nouns or pronouns in their works. When evaluating students' answers to the day-two exit question "Why are relative clauses important tools for effective writing?," I look at how well students explain that relative clauses are important because they add descriptive information that enhances the reader's understanding of the noun or pronoun being discussed.
- Students writing activities and corresponding reflections
  - I also recommend using students' work on the writing activities and corresponding reflections to assess their knowledge of relative clauses. To evaluate students' work on the passages they wrote, I assess whether or not they used a relative clause, if that relative clause describes a noun or pronoun, and if it provides descriptive detail about that noun or pronoun. When assessing students' reflections, I look at the level of detail and insight they provide when discussing the importance of the relative clause they used to the passage they created.

Notes

- What worked when teaching this lesson?
- What might you adapt or change the next time you teach it?

Reference

Alexander, K. (2014). *The crossover.* Houghton Mifflin Harcourt.

Lesson 7.3

Strong and Specific: Strong Verbs and Specific Nouns

Overview

This lesson focuses on strong verbs and specific nouns, tools that writers use to express information clearly and precisely. There are two class periods in this sequence. On the first day, students will learn what strong verbs and specific nouns are, see examples of them, examine how these concepts are used in published writing, and consider their impact. During the second day, students will review important information about strong verbs and specific nouns, apply them to their writing, and reflect on the importance of strong verbs and specific nouns to their works. At the conclusion of the instructional process, students will answer an exit question that asks them to consider the importance of strong verbs and specific nouns to writing.

Objectives

- Students will understand the characteristics of strong verbs and specific nouns.
- Students will learn the importance of strong verbs and specific nouns to effective writing.
- Students will apply strong verbs and specific nouns to their writing and reflect on the significance of doing so.

DOI: 10.4324/9781003466826-11

Time Frame

Two class periods.

Background Knowledge Required

Students should have general understandings of the concepts of nouns and verbs.

Materials Needed

- Figures 7.3.1–7.3.7, which are displayed in the lesson plan. They are also available in Appendix B: Reproducible Graphic Organizers and on the book's website.
- A projector, board, or piece of chart paper to display information.
- Paper students will use when writing.

Detailed Plan

Day One

1. Introduction

You'll open this instructional process by introducing students to the topics of strong verbs and specific nouns, sharing the key questions they'll consider during their first day of work on this topic, and providing the agenda for the day.

> We're going to explore two important grammatical concepts: strong verbs and specific nouns. Writers use these concepts as tools to express information clearly and precisely. Strong verbs are verbs that express actions in ways that readers can easily understand. Specific nouns are nouns that are concrete, clear, and easy for readers to visualize. Today's big questions are:
>
> - What are strong verbs and specific nouns?
> - Why are strong verbs and specific nouns important to writing?
>
> Let's look at our agenda for today:
>
> - Mini-lesson
> - Mentor text examples

- Mentor text discussion and analysis activities
- Exit question

I suggest displaying the big questions and agenda items while sharing them with students.

2. Mini-Lesson

You'll conduct a mini-lesson on important components of strong verbs and specific nouns. To do this, you'll discuss key features of these concepts, share examples of them, and talk about their importance to strong writing.

> In our mini-lesson on strong verbs and specific nouns, I'll introduce you to important information on these concepts; this will be the foundation for our work. You don't need to memorize this information now—we'll continue to discuss these ideas as we work on these concepts.
>
> Let's start by talking about what strong verbs and specific nouns are. You've heard of verbs and nouns, but these are verbs and nouns that express information clearly and precisely. Strong verbs express actions very clearly, and specific nouns are nouns that are easy for readers to understand. Let's look at some examples of strong verbs compared with weaker verbs that are less clear.

I recommend displaying this chart and discussing with students how readers can imagine the actions expressed in the strong verbs more clearly than in the weaker verbs.

"Now, we'll examine specific nouns compared to more general versions."

Strong Verb	Weaker Verb Comparison
Sprinted	Went
Shouted	Said
Devoured	Ate

Figure 7.3.1 Strong Verbs Compared with Weaker Verbs

Specific Noun	General Noun Comparison
Hockey	Sport
Pizza	Food
Hawk	Bird

Figure 7.3.2 Specific Nouns Compared with General Nouns

Grammatical Concepts	What Are Strong Verbs and Specific Nouns?	What Are Examples of Strong Verbs and Specific Nouns?	How Can Strong Verbs and Specific Nouns Look in Writing?	Why Are Strong Verbs and Specific Nouns Important?
Strong verbs and specific nouns	Strong verbs express actions in ways that readers can easily understand. Specific nouns are nouns that are concrete, clear, and easy for readers to visualize.	Strong Verb Examples: Sprinted Shouted Devoured Specific Noun Examples: Hockey Pizza Hawk	Strong Verb in Writing: The players **sprinted** onto the field. Specific Noun in Writing: We are excited to get home and eat **pizza**.	Strong verbs and specific nouns are important because they allow writers to express information clearly and precisely. Without them, writing would be more general and harder to understand.

Figure 7.3.3 Strong Verb and Specific Noun Information

Like with the previous chart, I recommend displaying these examples and talking with students about how readers can picture the specific nouns more clearly than the general ones.

"Now that we've looked at examples of these concepts and comparisons with other types of verbs and nouns, let's look at a chart that highlights key information about strong verbs and specific nouns."

I suggest displaying this chart while sharing its information with students.

3. Mentor Text Examples

Here, you'll share with students published examples of strong verbs and specific nouns. This will show students authentic examples of these concepts.

> We're going to now look at how strong verbs and specific nouns are used in published writing! I'm going to share with you two published sentences. The first one is from the book *Genesis Begins Again* by Alicia D. Williams (2019) and contains the strong verb 'rummages.' The second is from *Other Words for Home* by Jasmine Warga (2021) and contains the specific noun 'skyscrapers.'

I suggest displaying these sentences and reading them aloud. While reading them, I recommend pointing out the strong verb in the first sentence and the specific noun in the second sentence.

Published Example of Strong Verb	Published Example of Specific Noun
"Mama **rummages** through her dresser drawer" (Williams, 2019, p. 8). From *Genesis Begins Again* by Alicia D. Williams	"I asked him about the big **skyscrapers**…" (Warga, 2021, p. 3). From *Other Words for Home* by Jasmine Warga

Figure 7.3.4 Published Examples of Strong Verbs and Specific Nouns

Strong Verb Mentor Text	Revised Version with Strong Verb Replaced by Weaker Verb	Specific Noun Mentor Text	Revised Version with Specific Noun Replaced by General Noun
"Mama **rummages** through her dresser drawer" (Williams, 2019, p. 8).	Mama **looks** through her dresser drawer.	"I asked him about the big **skyscrapers**…" (Warga, 2021, p. 3).	I asked him about the big **buildings**.

Figure 7.3.5 Strong Verb and Specific Noun Mentor Texts Compared with Revised Versions

4. Mentor Text Discussion and Analysis Activities

In this section of the instructional process, you'll talk with students about the strong verb and specific noun mentor texts and conduct activities that will help them consider the importance of those concepts to the mentor texts in which they were used.

> Now that we've examined strong verb and specific noun mentor texts, we'll work together to consider why those strong verbs and specific nouns are so important to the mentor texts in which they were used. I'm going to show you a chart that compares the mentor text examples with revised versions. In the revised version of the strong verb sentence, the strong verb is replaced by a weaker verb. In the revised version of the specific noun sentence, the specific noun is replaced by a more general one.

I recommend displaying these examples on a projector screen and reading them aloud to students.

> Next, you'll talk with a partner about two reflection questions related to these sentences. The first question is: How is the sentence with a strong verb different from the one with a weaker verb? The second is: How is the sentence with a specific noun different from the one with a

Reflection Question One	Reflection Question Two
How is the sentence with a strong verb different from the one with a weaker verb?	How is the sentence with a specific noun different from the one with a general noun?

Figure 7.3.6 Strong Verb and Specific Noun Reflection Graphic Organizer

general noun? After you and your partner talk, I'll ask for volunteers to share ideas, and then I'll record responses on a graphic organizer.

I suggest displaying this graphic organizer and recording students' insights in the columns as they share.

5. Exit Question

To conclude this class period, students will answer an exit question on the significance of strong verbs and specific nouns.

In today's final activity, you'll write an answer to an exit question about strong verbs and specific nouns. Two volunteers will share their answers verbally; after that, I'll collect everyone's responses. The exit question is 'Why would writers use strong verbs and specific nouns?'

I like to display the question while reading it aloud. After students turn in their written responses, I recommend reviewing the answers to gauge students' understandings of the concept and inform future instruction.

Day Two

1. Introduction

To start the second day of work on strong verbs and specific nouns, you'll talk with students about how their work that day will build on the previous day's activities, discuss the day's key questions, and present the agenda.

> Excellent job yesterday on strong verbs and specific nouns! You learned key information about these concepts, examined published examples of them, considered the importance of those concepts to the published examples, and answered an exit question about why writers would use strong verbs and specific nouns. Today, we'll think even further about strong verbs and specific nouns. We'll first review key information about them. Afterward, we'll use strong verbs and specific nouns in our writing and reflect on their significance to those writings. We'll conclude with an exit question on the importance of strong verbs and specific nouns to writing. Our key questions for today are:
>
> ◆ How can we use strong verbs and specific nouns in our writing?
> ◆ How does using strong verbs and specific nouns impact our writing?
>
> Here is our agenda of activities for today:
>
> ◆ Review of strong verbs and specific nouns
> ◆ Writing activity
> ◆ Reflection
> ◆ Exit question

I recommend displaying these questions and this agenda as you share the information with students.

2. Review of Strong Verbs and Specific Nouns

Here, you'll review key information on strong verbs and specific nouns, such as the features, importance, and examples of these concepts discussed in the previous class.

> Let's review important information about strong verbs and specific nouns by looking together at a review chart on these concepts. This chart shares information about what strong verbs and specific nouns are, provides examples, discusses why they're important, and displays the published mentor texts we previously examined.

I suggest projecting this chart, reading its information aloud, and discussing any questions students have about strong verbs and specific nouns.

What Are Strong Verbs and Specific Nouns?	What Are Some Examples of Strong Verbs and Specific Nouns?	Why Are Strong Verbs and Specific Nouns Important?	What Are Published Examples of Strong Verbs and Specific Nouns?
Strong verbs express actions in ways that readers can easily understand. Specific nouns are nouns that are concrete, clear, and easy for readers to visualize.	Strong Verb Examples: Sprinted Shouted Devoured Specific Noun Examples: Hockey Pizza Hawk	Strong verbs and specific nouns are important because they allow writers to express information clearly and precisely. Without them, writing would be more general and harder to understand.	Published Example of Strong Verb: "Mama **rummages** through her dresser drawer" (Williams, 2019, p. 8). Published Example of Specific Noun: "I asked him about the big **skyscrapers**···" (Warga, 2021, p. 3).

Figure 7.3.7 Strong Verb and Specific Noun Review Information

3. *Writing Activity*

In this activity, students apply strong verbs and specific nouns to their writing. They compose one passage containing a strong verb and another containing a specific noun.

> Next, we'll use strong verbs and specific nouns in our writing! You'll write a sentence that uses an example of a strong verb and another that uses a specific noun. Before you write, I'll share examples that I created. The sentence I wrote that uses a strong verb is 'She <u>whispered</u> the secret to her friend.' I used the strong verb 'whispered' in this sentence. My specific noun sentence is 'We saw an <u>eagle</u> flying overhead.' Here, I used the specific noun 'eagle.'

I recommend writing your own sentences, one with a strong verb and another with a specific noun. You can then display these and share them with students.

"It's time for you to write! Create two sentences: one with a strong verb in it and another with a specific noun. Please underline the strong verb and the specific noun you use. Once you're done, you'll share your work with a partner; volunteers will share with the class."

As students write, I recommend moving around the room and checking on their uses of strong verbs and specific nouns.

"Now, turn to a partner and share with them the sentences you created. Identify the strong verb and specific noun you used."

While students share with partners, I circulate the classroom again, noting students' uses of these concepts and providing support.

"It's time for two volunteers to share the sentences they created and identify the strong verbs and specific nouns in them."

When students share their strong verbs and specific nouns, I recommend praising effective examples of these concepts and providing any useful explanations.

4. Reflection

Students now revisit the sentences they created in the preceding activity and reflect on the importance of the strong verbs and specific nouns they used.

> We're going to use the sentences you just created to reflect on strong verbs and specific nouns. You'll reread the sentences you wrote and think about the importance of the strong verbs and specific nouns you used. You'll write an answer to this question: 'Why are the strong verbs and specific nouns you used important to the sentences you wrote?'

I suggest displaying this question for students.

> Before you write, I'll share my reflection about the strong verbs and specific nouns I used. My strong verb sentence was 'She <u>whispered</u> the secret to her friend.' My specific noun sentence was 'We saw an <u>eagle</u> flying overhead.' For my reflection, I wrote 'The strong verb whispered was important to my strong verb sentence because it tells readers exactly how the subject communicated the secret to her friend. The specific noun eagle is important to my specific noun sentence because it lets readers know exactly what we saw.'

I recommend creating your own reflections about the strong verbs and specific nouns you used and sharing this with students to provide them with a model for their work.

"Revisit the strong verb and specific noun sentences you created and write a response to this question: 'Why are the strong verbs and specific nouns you used important to the sentences you wrote?'"

When students write, I like moving around the classroom to check on their progress and provide needed support.

"Now that you've written your reflection, share what you wrote with a partner and they'll share their work with you."

I suggest circulating the room while students share with their partners to hear what they say and give feedback.

"It's time for two volunteers to share their reflections verbally with the class. After that, everyone will turn in their reflections and their strong verb and specific noun sentences."

This is a great opportunity to call attention to strong reflections and clarify any misunderstandings.

5. Exit Question

This sequence ends with an exit question on the importance of strong verbs and specific nouns.

I'm going to ask you to write an answer to an exit question on strong verbs and specific nouns. After you write your answers, I'll ask for two volunteers to share and then I'll collect everyone's papers. The exit question is 'Why are strong verbs and specific nouns important tools for effective writing?'

I like to display the exit question for students. When volunteers share answers, I recommend noting strong insights and providing any needed clarification and information.

Differentiation Suggestions

This lesson can be differentiated in various ways:

- Students can examine additional mentor texts containing strong verbs and specific nouns to provide additional exposure to this concept in published work.
- Students can explore strong verb and specific noun mentor texts on a range of reading levels.
- Students can write multiple passages that contain strong verbs and specific nouns.
- Students can use multiple examples of these concepts in their passages.

Assessment

I recommend assessing students' knowledge of strong verbs and specific nouns in this lesson sequence in two ways:

- Students' exit question responses.
  - The exit question responses students create provide excellent opportunities to assess their understandings of strong verbs and

specific nouns. When evaluating students' responses to the first exit question, "Why would writers use strong verbs and specific nouns?," I assess how well they explain that writers use these concepts to express information clearly and precisely. When assessing students' answers to the second exit question, "Why are strong verbs and specific nouns important tools for effective writing?," I evaluate the detail and information students share when discussing the impact that these concepts have on effective writing.
- Students' written passages and reflections.
    - The passages students create that use strong verbs and specific nouns and the reflections that correspond with those passages are also useful when assessing students' understandings of these concepts. When assessing students' passages, I evaluate if they used strong verbs and specific nouns and if the examples they used align with the piece. When assessing their reflections, I evaluate if their responses show their understandings of these concepts and the information they provide.

Notes

- What worked when teaching this lesson?
- What might you adapt or change the next time you teach it?

References

Warga, J. (2021). *Other words for home.* Balzer + Bray.
Williams, A. (2019). *Genesis begins again.* Atheneum Books for Young Readers.

Lesson 7.4

Shades of Meaning: Connotation and Denotation

Overview

This lesson addresses connotation and denotation, important concepts for selecting and using language in writing. The instructional sequence spans two days. On the first day, students will learn what connotation and denotation are, explore words with similar denotations and different connotations, examine connotation-rich language in writing, and consider the importance of that language. On the second day, students will review information about connotation and denotation, apply connotation-rich language to their writing, and reflect on the significance of the connotations of the words they used. The instructional process concludes with students answering an exit question about the importance of understanding connotation and denotation to effective writing.

Objectives

- Students will understand the concepts of connotation and denotation.
- Students will learn the importance of connotation to effective writing.
- Students will apply their knowledge of connotation to writing and reflect on the significance of considering connotation when writing.

Time Frame

Two class periods.

Background Knowledge Required

No background knowledge is required for this lesson.

Materials Needed

- Figures 7.4.1–7.4.5. These figures are available in the lesson plan, in Appendix B: Reproducible Graphic Organizers, and on the book's website.
- A projector, board, or piece of chart paper for displaying information.
- Paper for students' written work.

Detailed Plan

Day One
1. Introduction
To begin this instructional process, you'll introduce the concepts of connotation and denotation, share the key questions for the first day of work on this topic, and provide the day's agenda.

> We're going to begin exploring the concepts of connotation and denotation. These are important topics for selecting and using language in writing. Today's big questions are:
>
> - What are the concepts of connotation and denotation?
> - Why is understanding the connotation and denotation of words important to writing?
>
> Let's look at our agenda for today:
>
> - Mini-lesson
> - Mentor text examples

- Mentor text discussions and analysis activities
- Exit question

I recommend displaying the big questions and agenda items while reading them aloud.

2. Mini-Lesson

Now, you'll teach a mini-lesson on connotation and denotation. To do this, you'll provide information about this topic, share examples of words with similar denotations and different connotations, and discuss the importance of understanding connotation and denotation.

> In this mini-lesson, I'll introduce you to some important ideas and information about connotation and denotation. This will be the starting point for the rest of our work on this concept. We'll continue to explore these ideas as we talk further about connotation and denotation.
>
> We'll begin by discussing what connotation and denotation are. The connotation of a word is the association we have with that word, such as a positive, negative, or neutral tone that we connect with it. The denotation of a word is its definition or literal meaning. Let's look at some word pairs that have similar denotations but different connotations.

I recommend displaying this information while discussing it with students.

"We'll now look at a chart that highlights key information about connotation and denotation."

I like to display this chart while discussing its information with students.

Word Pairs	Denotations	Connotations
Daring and Reckless	Daring and reckless have similar denotations because they both can be used to relate to boldness and fearlessness.	Daring has a positive connotation—it is often used to describe a brave action or person. Reckless has a negative connotation—it is often used to describe someone who acts in irresponsible ways.
Leisurely and Slow	Leisurely and slow have similar denotations because they both can be used to refer to something that is done in an unhurried way.	Leisurely has a positive connotation—it is often used to refer to something done in a relaxed way that is enjoyable. Slow has a negative connotation—it often refers to something that seems to take an especially long time.

Figure 7.4.1 Word Pairs with Similar Denotations but Different Connotations

Grammatical Concepts	What Is Connotation?	What Is Denotation?	Why Is Understanding Connotation and Denotation Important?
Connotation and denotation	The connotation of a word is the association we have with that word, such as a positive, negative, or neutral tone that we connect with it.	The denotation of a word is its definition or literal meaning.	Understanding a word's connotation and denotation is important because this knowledge helps us select the word that best goes with the message and tone we want to express when writing.

Figure 7.4.2 Connotation and Denotation Information

3. Mentor Text Example

Next, you'll share with students a published example of connotation-rich language. This provides an authentic example of how connotation relates to writing and communication.

> Let's look at how a published author uses a word with a specific connotation. In the book *The Absolute Value of Mike* by Katherine Erskine (2012), the author uses the connotation-rich word abandoned to maximize the effect of a statement. Erskine writes 'Moo nodded at an abandoned Exxon station' (p. 20).

When sharing this mentor text with students, I recommend displaying it so that the students can see the text as you read it.

4. Mentor Text Discussion and Analysis Activities

During this part of the lesson, you'll lead students through a discussion of the connotation-rich language used in the mentor text and conduct activities where students will consider the impact of the connotation-rich language the author used.

> Let's now think about the importance of the connotation-rich word abandoned to the mentor text passage we examined. First, let's consider the denotation of abandoned: its denotation is something that is left alone or not occupied. This word has a negative connotation: when a writer refers to something as abandoned, they are usually discussing something that is being described as empty in a negative way. A word with a similar denotation but a different connotation is empty. Something that is empty can also be left alone or not occupied, but this word does not have the same negative connotation. Its connotation is more neutral; we wouldn't usually use it to describe something in a

104 ♦ Shades of Meaning: Connotation and Denotation

Original Text	Revised Version with a Word with a Different Connotation
"Moo nodded at an **abandoned** Exxon station" (Erskine, 2012, p. 20).	Moo nodded at an **empty** Exxon station.

Figure 7.4.3 Original Text vs. Revised Version with Different Connotation

Reflection Question One	Reflection Question Two
How do you think the sentences are different?	Why do you think the author used the word abandoned in the original sentence?

Figure 7.4.4 Connotation Reflection Graphic Organizer

negative way like we'd do with the word abandoned. Let's look at a chart that compares the original passage from *The Absolute Value of Mike* with a new version in which abandoned is replaced with empty.

I suggest displaying this chart and reading the sentences aloud while students follow along.

In our next activity, you'll discuss with a partner two reflection questions related to these sentences. The first is: How do you think the two sentences are different? The second is: Why do you think the author used the word abandoned in the original sentence? After you discuss this information, I'll ask for volunteers to share their thoughts. I'll record information from your responses.

I like to display the graphic organizer and record students' insights on it when they share.

5. Exit Question
This class period concludes with an exit question on why writers think about connotations of words with similar denotations when writing.

> Now, you'll answer an exit question about connotations of words with similar denotations. You'll write your answer, two volunteers will share responses, and I'll collect everyone's work. The exit question is 'Why would writers think about the connotations of words with similar denotations while they write?'

I suggest displaying this question and reading it aloud. I also recommend evaluating students' written responses to evaluate their understandings of this concept. This information can inform your future instruction.

Day Two
1. Introduction
You'll begin the second day of work on connotation and denotation by talking with students about how the day's work builds on the first day, presenting the key questions, and sharing the agenda.

> Wonderful job working on connotation and denotation yesterday! In yesterday's class, you learned key information about these concepts, looked at examples of words with similar denotations and different connotations, examined a published example of connotation-rich language, reflected on that published work, and answered an exit question about these concepts. Today, we'll think even further about connotation and denotation. We'll start by reviewing key information about these concepts. Then, we'll apply our knowledge to our writing by using words with similar denotations and different connotations in passages we write. Finally, we'll answer an exit question on the importance of understanding connotation and denotation to effective writing. Today's key questions are:
>
> ◆ How can we apply our knowledge of connotation and denotation to our writing?

- Why are connotation and denotation important concepts for effective writing?

Here is today's agenda:

- Review of connotation and denotation
- Writing activity
- Reflection
- Exit question

I suggest displaying the questions and agenda items while presenting them to students.

2. Review of Connotation and Denotation

You'll review important information about connotation and denotation, such as what these terms mean, their importance, and examples of them.

"We're going to review key ideas about connotation and denotation by examining a chart on these topics. The chart provides information about what connotation and denotation are, discusses their importance, incorporates the published example we looked at yesterday, and includes the revised version of the published sentence containing a work with similar denotation but different connotation."

I recommend displaying this chart and reading its contents aloud. I also suggest discussing aspects of this topic that may have been challenging for students in the first lesson.

Grammatical Concepts	What Are Connotation and Denotation?	Why Is Understanding Connotation and Denotation Important?	Published Text Containing Language with a Specific Connotation	Revised Version with a Word with a Different Connotation but Similar Denotation
Connotation and Denotation	The **connotation** of a word is the association we have with that word, such as a positive, negative, or neutral tone. The **denotation** of a word is its definition or literal meaning.	Understanding a word's connotation and denotation is important because this knowledge helps us select the word that best goes with the message and tone we want to express when writing.	"Moo nodded at an **abandoned** Exxon station" (Erskine, 2012, p. 20).	Moo nodded at an **empty** Exxon station.

Figure 7.4.5 Connotation and Denotation Review Information

3. Writing Activity

Next, students complete a writing activity that focuses on connotation and denotation. In this activity, students create two sentences using words with different connotations and similar denotations.

> We're going to apply connotation and denotation to our writing! In this writing activity, you'll first create a sentence that uses a word with a specific connotation. Then, you'll rewrite the sentence, replacing that word with one that has a similar denotation but a different connotation. Before you write, I'll share an example. I wrote the sentence 'He has a collection of <u>vintage</u> baseball jerseys.' I then rewrote it as 'He has a collection of <u>outdated</u> baseball jerseys.' Vintage and outdated have similar denotations but different connotations.

I suggest writing your own example sentences for this activity, underlining the connotation-rich language, and displaying them for students.

> It's your turn! Create a sentence that uses a word with a specific connotation, rewrite it, replacing that word with another that has a similar denotation but a different connotation. Underline the connotation-rich words like I did with 'vintage' and 'outdated.'

While students write, I like to circulate the classroom and check in with them as they create these sentences and underline the words with different connotations and similar denotations.

> "Talk with a partner now and share the sentence you create, pointing out the words you underlined."

As students share their work with partners, I again move around the room, listening to the sentences they created and the words they underlined.

> "Now, two volunteers will share with the class the sentences they created, identifying the words they used with similar denotations and different connotations."

When students share these connotation-rich sentences, I suggest calling attention to strong work and providing additional explanations when necessary.

4. Reflection

In this reflective activity, students revisit the sentences they created and reflect on how using words with different connotations and similar denotations impacted the works.

> Now, we're going to do a reflective activity with the sentences you just wrote. You'll reread what you wrote in our last activity, review

the words in those sentences with similar denotations and different connotations you used, and write an answer to the question 'Why are the connotations of the words you used important to the sentences you wrote?'

I recommend displaying this question while sharing it with students.

Before you start, I'll share my reflection about the sentences I wrote. My sentences were 'He has a collection of <u>vintage</u> baseball jerseys' and 'He has a collection of <u>outdated</u> baseball jerseys.' In my reflection, I said 'The connotations of the words I used were important to my sentences because they impacted the tone in each sentence. The word 'vintage' creates a positive tone about the baseball jerseys; 'outdated' creates a negative tone.'

I suggest writing your own reflection about the connotations of the words you used and sharing it with your students.

"Look back at the sentences you created during our previous activity and write a reflection on the question 'Why are the connotations of the words you used important to the sentences you wrote?'"

As students write, I suggest circulating the classroom, monitoring their work, and providing support.

"Now, share your reflection with a partner and listen as they share theirs with you."

I like to move around the classroom while students share their reflections to hear their insights.

"Let's have two volunteers share their reflections out loud. Following that, everyone will turn in their reflections and the sentences you wrote for the writing activity."

When students share their reflections with the class, I recommend calling attention to any strong insights they share about connotations.

5. Exit Question

At the conclusion of this lesson sequence, students answer an exit question on the importance of connotation and denotation to effective writing.

For our final activity, you'll answer an exit question on connotation and denotation. You'll write your answers and then I'll ask for two volunteers to share their responses. Afterward, I'll collect everyone's papers. The exit question is 'Why is understanding connotation and denotation important to effective writing?'

I suggest displaying this exit question while students write their answers. When students share, I suggest praising strong points and building on any statements that need further explanation.

Differentiation Suggestions

This lesson can be differentiated in numerous ways:

- ◆ Students can read additional mentor text examples of connotation-rich language, providing them with increased opportunities to see the role of connotation in published writing.
- ◆ Students can examine mentor texts on a range of reading levels; connotation-rich language can be found in texts on a variety of reading levels.
- ◆ Students can write and revise multiple passages in the writing activity.
- ◆ Students can create and revise multiple examples of connotation-rich language in the writing activity.

Assessment

I suggest assessing students' understandings of connotation and denotation in these ways:

- ◆ Students' exit question answers.
  - ◇ Students' answers to the two exit questions during this instructional sequence are great ways to assess their understandings of connotation and denotation. When assessing students' responses to the first exit question, "Why would writers think about the connotations of words with similar denotations while they write?," I evaluate how well students explain that writers would consider this topic in order to use the language that best matches their intended tone. When assessing students' answers to the day two exit question "Why is understanding connotation and denotation important to effective writing?," I evaluate the information and detail students share when describing why both of these concepts are important to the message and tone in a piece of writing.

- The written passages and corresponding reflections students create.
  - The sentences that students write during the writing activity and the corresponding reflections they write also provide great opportunities to assess students' understandings of connotation and denotation. When assessing students' written passages, I evaluate if the words students use and underline have similar denotations but different connotations. When assessing their reflections, I look at how well students explain the importance of the connotations of the identified words to the meaning and information in the sentences.

Notes

- What worked when teaching this lesson?
- What might you adapt or change the next time you teach it?

Reference

Erskine, K. (2012). *The absolute value of Mike*. Puffin Books.

Lesson 7.5

Intentional Sentence Construction: Simple, Compound, and Complex Sentences

Overview

This lesson focuses on simple, compound, and complex sentences, three important sentence constructions that authors use in their writing. There are two days of instruction in this sequence. On day one, students will learn the features of simple, compound, and complex sentences; look at examples of them; see how these sentence types are used in published writing; and consider the benefits of their use. During day two, students will review key information about simple, compound, and complex sentences; create examples of them; and reflect on the benefits of each sentence type they created. The lesson sequence ends with an exit question that asks students to comment on the importance of simple, compound, and complex sentences to effective writing.

Objectives

- Students will learn the features of simple, compound, and complex sentences.
- Students will understand the importance of simple, compound, and complex sentences to strong writing.
- Students will create examples of simple, compound, and complex sentences and reflect on the impact of each sentence type.

Time Frame

Two class periods.

Background Knowledge Required

No background knowledge is required for this lesson.

Materials Needed

- Figures 7.5.1–7.5.8. These figures can be found in the lesson plan, in Appendix B: Reproducible Graphic Organizers, and on the book's website.
- A projector, board, or piece of chart paper for displaying information.
- Paper for students to use.

Detailed Plan

Day One
1. Introduction
Here, you'll introduce the concepts of simple, compound, and complex sentences; share the key questions students will consider in their first day working on these topics; and go over the day's agenda.

> We're going to work on simple, compound, and complex sentences, three sentence types that writers use to express ideas and share information in intentional and purposeful ways. Today, we'll focus on these key questions:
>
> - What are simple, compound, and complex sentences?
> - Why are simple, compound, and complex sentences important to effective writing?
>
> Here is the agenda for today's work on these sentence types:
>
> - Mini-lesson
> - Mentor text examples

- Mentor text discussion and analysis activities
- Exit question

I recommend displaying the day's key questions and agenda while sharing this information.

2. Mini-Lesson

You'll conduct a mini-lesson on simple, compound, and complex sentences. To do this, you'll discuss key features of these sentence types, share examples of them, and talk about their importance.

> In this mini-lesson on simple, compound, and complex sentences, I'll introduce you to important information on these sentence types. We'll refer back to these ideas as we continue to work on this topic.
>
> First, let's talk about what each of these sentence types are. Simple sentences are made up of one independent clause. An independent clause contains a subject and verb and expresses a complete thought. For example, the statement 'Kate ran the race' is an independent clause and is an example of a simple sentence. Simple sentences are important tools for writing because they express information directly and clearly. Let's look at a chart that summarizes information about simple sentences.

I suggest displaying this chart and sharing its information with students.

> Compound sentences contain two or more independent clauses joined by a coordinator. For example, if we turned our simple sentence 'Kate ran the race' into a compound sentence, it could read 'Kate ran the race, and Jake cheered her on.' This sentence contains two independent clauses that are joined by a coordinator. There are different kinds of coordinators we can use in compound sentences. One of these is a coordinating conjunction, which can be used with

Sentence Type	Description	Example	Importance to Effective Writing
Simple sentence	A simple sentence is made up of one independent clause.	Kate ran the race.	Simple sentences are important to effective writing because they express information directly and clearly.

Figure 7.5.1 Key Information about Simple Sentences

Sentence Type	Description	Examples	Importance to Effective Writing
Compound sentence	A compound sentence is made up of two or more independent clauses joined by a coordinator, such as a comma and coordinating conjunction or a semicolon.	Kate ran the race, and Jake cheered her on. Kate ran the race; Jake cheered her on.	Compound sentences are important to effective writing because they connect ideas and help the flow of a piece of writing.

Figure 7.5.2 Key Information about Compound Sentences

commas to join independent clauses. These conjunctions are the words *for, and, nor, but, or, yet,* and *so*. For example, the previously-used sentence 'Kate ran the race, and Jake cheered her on' uses a comma and the coordinating conjunction 'and.' Another coordinator often used to link independent clauses in compound sentences is a semicolon. We can use semicolons in place of coordinating conjunctions to connect independent clauses, such as 'Kate ran the race; Jake cheered her on.' Compound sentences are important tools for strong writing because they connect ideas and help the flow of a piece of writing. Let's check out a chart that highlights ideas about compound sentences.

I recommend projecting this chart and reading it aloud.

Complex sentences contain an independent clause and at least one dependent clause. A dependent clause contains a subject and verb, but, unlike an independent clause, cannot stand on its own as a sentence. An example of a complex sentence is 'Since she ran the race, Kate was very tired.' In this sentence, 'Kate was very tired' is an independent clause, and 'Since she ran the race' is a dependent clause. The independent clause can stand on its own as a sentence; the dependent clause can't. Some words that often begin dependent clauses are *although, because, if, since, until, after, when,* and *where*. Complex sentences are useful tools for effective writing because they include background information and context that helps the reader understand what's taking place. We'll now look at information about complex sentences.

I suggest displaying this chart and reading its contents for students.

Sentence Type	Description	Example	Importance to Effective Writing
Complex sentence	A complex sentence is made up of an independent clause and at least one dependent clause.	Since she ran the race, Kate was very tired.	Complex sentences are important to effective writing because the background information and context they provide helps the reader's understanding.

Figure 7.5.3 Key Information about Complex Sentences

Published Simple Sentence Example	Published Compound Sentence Example	Published Complex Sentence Example
"We woke up at a little before seven" (Hiranandani, 2018, p. 1). From *The Night Diary* by Veera Hiranandani	"The diner's packed with families tonight, so the show should be a hoot" (Crowder, 2022, p. 4). From *Mazie* by Melanie Crowder	"When they got close to the ramp, Papa hunkered down behind the last of the crates" (Gratz, 2017, p. 37). From *Refugee* by Alan Gratz

Figure 7.5.4 Published Examples of Simple, Compound, and Complex Sentences

3. *Mentor Text Examples*

Now, you'll share with your students published examples of simple, compound, and complex sentences. This shows how these sentence types are used in authentic writing.

"We're going to look at how published authors use simple, compound, and complex sentences in their works. I'm going to share with you published examples of each of these sentence types."

I suggest displaying these sentences and reading them aloud. While reading them, I recommend talking with students about the reasons that each of these sentences is an example of its particular sentence type.

4. *Mentor Text Discussion and Analysis Activities*

You'll lead students through activities that will help them think about the benefits associated with using each of the sentence types found in the mentor text examples. This will help develop students' understandings of how authors use each of these sentence types intentionally in their work.

> We've seen published examples of simple, compound, and complex sentences. Now we'll discuss the benefits of using each of these sentence types. We'll re-examine each mentor text example, and you'll reflect on the benefits associated with using that sentence type. First, I'll display our simple sentence example. I'll ask you to talk with a partner about the benefits of using that simple sentence. Then, we'll record some responses in the chart I'll display.

116 ◆ Intentional Sentence Construction: Simple, Compound, and Complex Sentences

Simple Sentence Mentor Text	Benefits of Using This Sentence Type
"We woke up at a little before seven" (Hiranandani, 2018, p. 1).	

Figure 7.5.5 Simple Sentence Benefits Analysis Chart

Compound Sentence Mentor Text	Benefits of Using This Sentence Type
"The diner's packed with families tonight, so the show should be a hoot" (Crowder, 2022, p. 4).	

Figure 7.5.6 Compound Sentence Benefits Analysis Chart

I suggest displaying this chart, reading the sentence aloud, and asking students to talk with partners about what they think some benefits are of using a simple sentence in this situation. While students talk with each other, I like to move around the room to listen to and support their conversations. I then ask for volunteers to share ideas and record them on the chart. I look for responses that highlight how the simple sentence allows the writer to express information in a clear and direct way.

> Now, let's do similar work with our compound sentence mentor text. I'll display the compound sentence example and ask you to talk with a partner about the benefits of using that sentence type. We'll then record some responses in the chart

I recommend displaying this information, reading aloud the sentence, and then asking students to talk together about the benefits of using a compound sentence here. I circulate the classroom while students talk, listening to and supporting their work. I then record ideas that volunteers share on the chart. When students share, I especially look for comments that call attention to how the compound sentence connects ideas and enhances the flow of the sentence.

> "Next, we'll focus on our complex sentence mentor text. We'll look at the example of a complex sentence. Then, you'll talk to a partner about the benefits of using that sentence type. I'll write some responses on this chart."

Complex Sentence Mentor Text	Benefits of Using This Sentence Type
"When they got close to the ramp, Papa hunkered down behind the last of the crates" (Gratz, 2017, p. 37).	

Figure 7.5.7 Complex Sentence Benefits Analysis Chart

You'll share this chart with students and read the example aloud before asking students to talk with partners about the benefits of using a complex sentence in this situation. When students talk, I recommend moving around the classroom and providing any needed assistance. After that, I ask volunteers to share, recording insights on the chart. I look for responses that highlight how the complex sentence helps the author provide background information that can be useful to readers.

5. Exit Question

This instructional day concludes with students answering an exit question on simple, compound, and complex sentences.

> Now, you'll write an answer to an exit question about simple, compound, and complex sentences. I'll ask for two volunteers to share their answers aloud and then I'll collect everyone's work. The exit question is 'Why would writers use simple, compound, and complex sentences in their writing?'

After students turn in their answers, I suggest reviewing them to monitor their understandings. This information can inform future instruction.

Day Two
1. Introduction

To begin the second day on simple, compound, and complex sentences, you'll explain how students' work that day will build on the previous one, discuss the day's questions, and share the agenda.

> Great work yesterday on simple, compound, and complex sentences! You learned about these topics, saw published examples of them, reflected on the benefits of the published authors using each of these sentence types, and answered an exit question about why authors use these sentence types in their writing. Today, we'll work

on these sentence types even further. We'll review key information about them, create our examples of each sentence type, reflect on the benefits of using each of these types, and answer an exit question on the importance of simple, compound, and complex sentences to writing. Today's key questions are:

- How can we use simple, compound, and complex sentences in our writing?
- How does our writing benefit from using these sentence types?

Here is our agenda for today:

- Review of simple, compound, and complex sentences
- Writing activity
- Reflection
- Exit question

I suggest displaying the key questions and agenda while sharing them with students.

2. Review of Simple, Compound, and Complex Sentences

You'll review key information about simple, compound, and complex sentences, highlighting key ideas discussed the previous day.

Sentence Type	Description	Published Example	Importance to Effective Writing
Simple sentence	A simple sentence is made up of one independent clause.	"We woke up at a little before seven" (Hiranandani, 2018, p. 1).	Simple sentences are important to effective writing because they express information directly and clearly.
Compound sentence	A compound sentence is made up of two or more independent clauses joined by a coordinator, such as a comma and coordinating conjunction or a semicolon.	"The diner's packed with families tonight, so the show should be a hoot" (Crowder, 2022, p. 4).	Compound sentences are important to effective writing because they connect ideas and help the flow of a piece of writing.
Complex sentence	A complex sentence is made up of an independent clause and at least one dependent clause.	"When they got close to the ramp, Papa hunkered down behind the last of the crates" (Gratz, 2017, p. 37).	Complex sentences are important to effective writing because the background information and context they provide helps the reader's understanding.

Figure 7.5.8 Simple, Compound, and Complex Sentence Review Information

"Let's review important information about simple, compound, and complex sentences by looking at a review chart. It provides the following information about each sentence type: a description of it, the published example we saw in our last class, and information about its importance to effective writing."

I recommend projecting this chart, reading its contents aloud, and discussing any questions students have about these sentence types.

3. Writing Activity

Students now apply their knowledge of simple, compound, and complex sentences to their writing by creating examples of each of these sentence types.

> Now, we'll use these sentence types in our writing. You'll create a simple sentence, a compound sentence, and a complex sentence. Before you start, I'll share with you the examples I created. My simple sentence is 'The tired dog rested on the floor.' My compound sentence is 'The tired dog rested on the floor, but the cat jumped on the couch.' My complex sentence is 'Because he was exhausted from a long walk, the tired dog rested on the floor.' I made all of these sentences about a similar topic—you can do something similar when you create your own, but it's not required.

I suggest creating your own examples of each of these sentence types, displaying them, and sharing them with students.

"You'll create your own examples of simple, compound, and complex sentences. I'll come around and check in with you while you work."

As students create their sentences, I like to circulate the classroom, monitoring their progress and providing relevant praise and support.

"Good job working on those sentences! Let's take two volunteers to share the sentences they created and identify the sentence types."

When students share their sentences, I recommend praising strong examples of these sentence types and providing any needed clarification.

4. Reflection

Here, students revisit the sentences they created in the writing activity and reflect on the benefits of using each sentence type.

"We're going to use the sentences you just wrote for a reflective activity. You'll re-read the sentences and then answer the following question for each sentence you wrote: 'What is a benefit of using that sentence type?'"

I recommend displaying this question for students.

Before you do this, I'll share my reflections on the sentences I created. For the simple sentence 'The tired dog rested on the floor,' I said 'A benefit of using a simple sentence here is that the sentence expresses information about the dog clearly and directly.' For the compound sentence 'The tired dog rested on the floor, but the cat jumped on the couch,' I reflected 'A benefit of using a compound sentence here is that it connects the information about the cat and the dog.' For the complex sentence 'Because he was exhausted from a long walk, the tired dog rested on the floor,' I wrote 'A benefit of using this complex sentence is that the sentence gives background information that helps the reader understand.'

I suggest reflecting on the benefits of the simple, compound, and complex sentences you created and sharing these reflections with students to provide them with models.

"Look back at the simple, compound, and complex sentences you wrote and answer the question 'What is a benefit of using that sentence type?' for each sentence."

While students write, I circulate the classroom to check in on their progress, sharing support and encouragement.

"Let's now have two volunteers share their sentences and reflections verbally. Then, everyone will hand in their reflections and the sentences they created."

When students share, I suggest calling attention to strong points and addressing any confusion.

5. Exit Question

This sequence concludes with an exit question on the importance of simple, compound, and complex sentences.

We'll end with an exit question on simple, compound, and complex sentences. You'll write your answers, two volunteers will share, and I'll collect them. The exit question is 'Why are simple, compound, and complex sentences important tools for effective writing?'

I suggest displaying the exit question. When students answer, I recommend praising strong statements and providing any further explanation.

Differentiation Suggestions

This lesson can be differentiated in several ways:

- ◆ Students can examine additional mentor text examples of simple, compound, and complex sentences.

- Students can read examples of these sentence types on a variety of reading levels.
- Students can write multiple examples of these sentence types.

Assessment

I suggest assessing students' knowledge of simple, compound, and complex sentences in these ways:

- Students' exit question responses.
  - Students' responses to both of the exit questions in this instructional sequence provide insight into their knowledge of simple, compound, and complex sentences. When assessing students' responses to the day-one question "Why would writers use simple, compound, and complex sentences in their writing?," I evaluate how well students explain that writers use these tools purposefully to achieve the benefits associated with each sentence type. When evaluating students' responses to the day-two question "Why are simple, compound, and complex sentences important tools for effective writing?," I look at how well students explain that each of these sentence types can enhance writing in its own way.
- Students' written sentences and reflections.
  - The examples that students create and their corresponding reflections also provide important assessment data. I assess their sentences to determine if they accurately create examples of each sentence type and support them if they have trouble with this. I evaluate students' responses to assess if they understand the benefits of each type.

Notes

- What worked when teaching this lesson?
- What might you adapt or change the next time you teach it?

References

Crowder, M. (2022). *Mazie*. Viking Books for Young Readers.
Gratz, A. (2017). *Refugee*. Scholastic.
Hiranandani, V. (2018). *The night diary*. Kokila.

SECTION THREE

Lesson Plans Recommended for the Eighth-Grade English Classroom

Lesson 8.1
Purposeful Structures: Active and Passive Voices

Overview

This lesson addresses the concepts of active and passive voices, two ways that writers can structure statements. The sequence spans two days. On day one, students will learn what the active and passive voices are, consider their uses, examine published examples of them, and analyze those examples. On day two, students will review information about the active and passive voices, create examples of them, and reflect on the effects of using them. The process concludes with an exit question about how using the active and passive voices can be important to students' future writing.

Objectives

- Students will understand the features of the active and passive voices.
- Students will learn the importance of the active and passive voices to effective writing.
- Students will use the active and passive voices in their writing and reflect on the effects of doing so.

Time Frame

Two class periods.

DOI: 10.4324/9781003466826-15

Background Knowledge Required

A knowledge of the topics of direct objects, forms of the verb 'be,' and past participles can help students understand the features of the active and passive voices.

Materials Needed

- Figures 8.1.1–8.1.5, which can be found in the lesson plan, in Appendix B: Reproducible Graphic Organizers, and on the book's website.
- A projector, board, or piece of chart paper for displaying information.
- Paper for students to use.

Detailed Plan

Day One
1. Introduction
To begin this sequence, you'll introduce students to the topics of the active and passive voices, share the key questions they'll consider during their first day learning about these concepts, and provide the day's agenda.

> Let's begin our exploration of the active and passive voices. These are two ways that authors can structure statements in their writing. The key questions we'll consider today are:
>
> - What are the active and passive voices?
> - What are benefits of using the active and passive voices?
>
> Let's look at our agenda for day:
>
> - Mini-lesson
> - Mentor text examples
> - Mentor text discussion
> - Exit question

I recommend displaying these questions and agenda items while reading them aloud.

2. Mini-Lesson

You'll conduct a mini-lesson on the active and passive voices. To do so, you'll discuss the features of the active and passive voices, share examples, and explain why writers use them.

> In this mini-lesson, I'll introduce you to key information on the active and passive voices. Let's start with the active voice. In an active voice sentence, the subject of the sentence is performing the action. For example, the sentence 'Rob fixed the computer' is in the active voice—Rob is the subject of the sentence and is also performing the action.
>
> Now, let's talk about the passive voice, which is structured differently. In a passive voice sentence, the subject is not performing the action. Instead, the subject is the person or thing on which the action was performed. For example, a passive voice version of 'Rob fixed the computer' could be 'The computer fixed by Rob.' In a passive voice sentence, we can also remove the person or thing performing an action and say 'The computer was fixed.' In these passive voice sentences, 'the computer' is the subject.
>
> To change an active voice sentence to a passive one, we take the direct object in the active voice sentence, make it the subject, and change the verb slightly—we put a form of the verb 'be' in front of the main verb and put the main verb in its past participle form. That's how we turned 'Rob fixed the computer' into 'The computer was fixed by Rob.'"
>
> Writers use each of these voices for different reasons. The active voice puts more emphasis on the person or thing performing the action, while the passive voice focuses more on the action that was performed and the thing impacted by the action. The active voice is more direct and clear, and the passive voice can be less direct and wordier. However, each one can be used for a particular purpose.
>
> Let's take a look at a chart that summarizes key information about the active and passive voices.

I recommend displaying this chart while reading its information aloud.

Sentence Types	Descriptions	Examples	Why They're Used
Active voice	The subject of the sentence is performing the action.	Rob fixed the computer.	The active voice puts more emphasis on the person or thing performing the action.
Passive voice	The subject is not performing the action. The subject is the person or thing on which the action was performed.	The computer was fixed by Rob.	The passive voice focuses more on the action that was performed and the thing impacted by the action.

Figure 8.1.1 Active and Passive Voice Information

3. Mentor Text Examples

You'll share with students published examples of the active and passive voices. These examples will provide students with authentic uses of these concepts.

"The next step in our work is to look at how the active and passive voices are used in published writing. I'll share with you a published example of the active voice from the book *XOXO* by Axie Oh (2021) and a published example of the passive voice from *A Pho Love Story* (2021) by Loan Le."

I recommend displaying these sentences and reading them aloud. While doing this, I suggest talking with students about why each sentence is an example of its particular voice.

4. Mentor Text Discussion and Analysis Activities

During this part of the instructional process, you'll talk with students about the active and passive voice mentor texts and help them consider the benefits of the voice used in each example.

Now that we've looked at active and passive voice mentor texts, we're going to work together to consider the benefits of each voice to the sentence in which it was used. I'll show you a chart that compares each mentor text example with a revised version of the sentence rewritten in the other voice. The active voice sentence is rewritten as possible passive voice versions and the passive voice sentence is rewritten as an active voice version.

Published Active Voice Example	Published Passive Voice Example
"I stuff the note deep into my pocket" (Oh, 2021, p. 6). From *XOXO* by Axie Oh	"The article was written" (Le, 2021, p. 348). From *A Pho Love Story* by Loan Le

Figure 8.1.2 Published Examples of the Active and Passive Voices

Active Voice Mentor Text	Rewritten in Passive Voice	Passive Voice Mentor Text	Rewritten in Active Voice
"I stuff the note deep into my pocket" (Oh, 2021, p. 6).	The note is stuffed deep into my pocket by me. Or: The note is stuffed deep into my pocket.	"The article was written" (Le, 2021, p. 348).	Someone wrote the article.

Figure 8.1.3 Active and Passive Voice Mentor Texts Compared with Revised Versions

Reflection Question One	Reflection Question Two
What is a benefit of using the active voice in the active voice mentor text?	What is a benefit of using the passive voice in the passive voice mentor text?

Figure 8.1.4 Active and Passive Voice Reflection Graphic Organizer

I suggest displaying this chart and reading its information aloud.

> Next, you'll talk to a partner about two reflection questions about the mentor text sentences. The first question is: What is a benefit of using the active voice in the active voice mentor text? The second is: What is a benefit of using the passive voice in the passive voice mentor text? After you discuss with your partner, I'll ask for volunteers to share, and I'll record ideas on a graphic organizer.

I recommend displaying this graphic organizer and recording students' insights on it as they share.

5. Exit Question

This class period concludes with students answering an exit question on the significance of the active and passive voices.

> For our final activity of today, you'll write an answer to an exit question about the active and passive voices. After you write, I'll ask for two volunteers to share verbally and then I'll collect all written responses. The exit question is 'Why would writers use the active and passive voices?'

I suggest displaying this question while reading it aloud. After students submit their written responses, I examine their answers to monitor their understandings. If there are any misunderstandings, I address those the next day.

Day Two

1. Introduction

To begin day two of instruction on the active and passive voices, you'll discuss with students how this day's work will build on the previous day's activities, introduce the day's key questions, and present the agenda.

> Great work on the active and passive voices yesterday! You learned important information about these topics, looked at published examples of them, reflected on those published examples, and answered an exit question about why writers would use the active and passive voices. Today, we'll explore the active and passive voices even further. First, we'll review key information about them. Then, we'll create active and passive voice sentences and reflect on the benefits of using these sentence types. We'll finish with an exit question on how using the active and passive voices can be important to our future writing. Today's key questions are:
>
> - How can we use the active and passive voices in our writing?
> - How can using the active and passive voices be important to our writing?
>
> Our agenda of activities for today is:
>
> - Review of active and passive voices
> - Writing activity
> - Reflection
> - Exit question

I suggest displaying the questions and agenda items while sharing them with students.

2. Review of Active and Passive Voices

In this section, you'll review information about the active and passive voices discussed in the previous day's class, such as their descriptions, examples of them, and the reasons they're used.

"To review important information about the active and passive voices, we'll look together at a review chart about these topics. This chart contains descriptions of the active and passive voices, the published mentor texts we previously explored, and explanations of why they're used."

I recommend projecting this chart and reading its information aloud. If students showed any misunderstandings or confusion the previous day, this is a good time to address those.

Sentence Types	Descriptions	Published Mentor Text Examples	Why They're Used
Active voice	The subject of the sentence is performing the action.	"I stuff the note deep into my pocket" (Oh, 2021, p. 6).	The active voice puts more emphasis on the person or thing performing the action.
Passive voice	The subject is not performing the action. The subject is the person or thing on which the action was performed.	"The article was written" (Le, 2021, p. 348).	The passive voice focuses more on the action that was performed and the thing impacted by the action.

Figure 8.1.5 Active and Passive Voice Review Information

3. Writing Activity

During this activity, students will apply their knowledge of the active and passive voices by creating an example of a sentence in the active voice and an example in the passive voice.

> Now, we'll put our understandings of these topics into action in our writing! You'll create a sentence in the active voice, and you'll create another in the passive voice. Before you write, I'll share the examples I created. My active voice sentence is 'Sawyer caught the baseball.' My passive voice sentence is 'The pie was baked by Joyce.'

I suggest creating your own active and passive voice examples, displaying them, and sharing them aloud with students.

"Now, it's time for you to create your own. Write an example of an active voice and a passive voice sentence. After you do that, I'll ask you to share your work with a partner."

While students create their sentences, I circulate the classroom to check in on their progress and provide support.

"Good job creating those sentences. Talk with a partner and share the active and passive voice sentences you wrote."

As students share with partners, I recommend again moving around the classroom, listening to their examples and giving feedback.

"Let's have two volunteers share with us the active and passive voice sentences they wrote."

When volunteers share their examples, I comment on strong examples of the active and passive voices. If student work conveys any confusion, I provide relevant clarification.

4. Reflection

In this activity, students revisit the active and passive voice sentences in the writing activity and reflect on the benefits of using each of these voices.

> We'll now use the active and passive voice sentences we created in our last activity to reflect on the benefits of the active and passive voices. First, you'll re-read the active voice sentence you created and use it to write brief reflections on two questions: 'What is a benefit of using the active voice in the active voice sentence you wrote?' and 'What is a benefit of using the passive voice in the passive voice sentence you wrote?'

I suggest displaying these questions while sharing them with students.

> I'll share my reflections about the sentences I wrote. When I responded to the reflection question regarding my active voice sentence 'Sawyer caught the baseball,' I wrote 'A benefit of using the active voice here is that it focuses the sentence on the fact that Sawyer specifically was the one who caught the baseball. It emphasizes that he did it.' When I answered the passive voice reflection about my passive voice sentence 'The pie was baked by Joyce,' I said 'A benefit of using the passive voice in this sentence is that it puts emphasis on the pie. This could be useful if I really wanted to focus the reader's attention on the pie in this sentence.'

I recommend writing your own reflections about the active and passive voice sentences you created and sharing those reflections with students to provide them examples.

> Now, revisit the active and passive voice sentences you created and write reflections on the questions 'What is a benefit of using the active voice in the active voice sentence you wrote?' and 'What is a benefit of using the passive voice in the passive voice sentence you wrote?'

As students write, I move around the room to monitor their progress and provide support.

> "Please share with a partner the reflections you created; they'll then do the same."

I like to again circulate the classroom while students share with partners. I praise strong responses and encourage students to further develop statements when relevant.

> "I'll ask for two volunteers to share their reflections with the class. Then, all students will turn in their reflections and their active and passive voice sentences."

When volunteers share, I call attention to especially insightful responses and provide any needed elaboration on statements that can benefit from additional explanation.

5. Exit Question

To conclude this lesson sequence, students answer an exit question on the importance of the active and passive voices.

We'll conclude our work on the active and passive voices with an exit question. Please write your answer; I'll ask for two volunteers to share verbally and then I'll collect everyone's work. The exit question is 'How can using the active and passive voices be important to your future writing?'

I recommend displaying the exit question while reading it. When students share responses, I like to note strong points and elaborate when relevant.

Differentiation Suggestions

This lesson can be differentiated in a variety of ways:

- ◆ Students can read more active and passive voice mentor texts, increasing their experiences with these concepts in published writing.
- ◆ Students can explore active and passive voice mentor texts on varying reading levels.
- ◆ Students can create multiple examples of the active and passive voices and use all of them in their reflections.

Assessment

I suggest assessing students' knowledge of the active and passive voices in this instructional process in two ways:

- ◆ Students' exit questions.
  - ◇ Students' answers to the two exit questions can provide important insights into their knowledge of the active and passive voices. When evaluating students' work on the first day's exit question,

"Why would writers use the active and passive voices?," I assess how well they explain that writers would use each voice in ways that correspond with its benefits, such as how each voice can emphasize a different aspect of a sentence. When assessing responses to the day-two exit question "How can using the active and passive voices be important to your future writing?," I evaluate how well students explain that using these voices can be important because they can help students write in purposeful ways that align with their intended message and focus.
- Students' written examples and reflections.
    - The examples of active and passive voice sentences students create and the corresponding reflections also help us assess students' knowledge of these topics. When assessing students' examples, I look to see if they created sentences in the active and passive voices. When evaluating their reflections, I assess if their statements demonstrate knowledge of the benefit of each voice in the examples they created.

Notes

- What worked when teaching this lesson?
- What might you adapt or change the next time you teach it?

References

Le, L. (2021). *A pho love story*. Simon and Schuster.
Oh, A. (2021). *XOXO*. HarperTeen.

Lesson 8.2

Time for a Break: Punctuation that Indicates a Pause or Break

Overview

This two-day lesson addresses how punctuation, such as commas, dashes, and ellipses, can be used to indicate a brief pause or break in a sentence. On day one, students learn what it means to use punctuation to indicate a pause or break, explore punctuation marks used for this purpose, examine how this concept is used in published works, and consider the impact of using it. On day two, students will review this topic, apply the concept to their writing, and reflect on the significance of using it. To conclude the process, students will answer an exit question about how using punctuation to indicate a pause or break can be important to their writing.

Objectives

- Students will understand the concept of using punctuation to indicate a pause or break.
- Students will learn the importance of using punctuation to indicate a pause or break.
- Students will apply the concept of using punctuation to indicate a pause or break and reflect on the significance of doing so.

Time Frame

Two class periods.

Background Knowledge Required

Students should be familiar with commas, dashes, and ellipses.

Materials Needed

- Figures 8.2.1–8.2.11. They are displayed in the lesson plan, in Appendix B: Reproducible Graphic Organizer, and on the book's website.
- A projector, board, or piece of chart paper for displaying information.
- Paper for students to use.

Detailed Plan

Day One
1. Introduction
You'll introduce students to the concept of using punctuation to indicate a pause or break, share the key questions for the first day of work on the topic, and display the day's agenda.

> We're going to be talking about using punctuation to indicate a pause or break. When writers want their readers to briefly pause or break while reading a sentence, they use punctuation, such as commas, dashes, and ellipses, to show this. Today's key questions are:
>
> - What does it mean to use punctuation to indicate a pause or break?
> - Why is using punctuation to indicate a pause or break important to effective writing?
>
> Our agenda for today is:
>
> - Mini-lesson
> - Mentor text examples

- Mentor text discussion and analysis activities
- Exit question

I recommend projecting the key questions and agenda items while reading them aloud.

2. Mini-Lesson

You'll conduct a mini-lesson on using punctuation to indicate a pause or break by discussing this topic, sharing information about punctuation used for this purpose, providing examples, and describing its importance to effective writing.

> I'll introduce you to the idea of using punctuation to indicate a pause or break. This will establish the foundation for our work on this topic, which we'll discuss in more depth. Let's talk about what it means to use punctuation to indicate a pause or break: when writers want their readers to take a pause or break in a sentence, they express this through punctuation. Three punctuation marks that can be used for this purpose are commas, dashes, and ellipses. Let's look at examples of how these punctuation marks can be used to indicate a pause or break.

I suggest displaying these sentences, reading them aloud, and pointing out the relevant punctuation that is used to indicate a pause or break.

> Using punctuation to indicate a pause or break in a sentence is important to good writing because it helps readers understand what they're reading and allows them to read the work in the way the writer intended. These punctuation marks can separate pieces of information, build suspense, or show that a character or author has paused before continuing a statement. Without this type of punctuation in a sentence, readers wouldn't know when to pause in a sentence. This would make the sentence harder to comprehend, and it wouldn't let them read the work the way the author meant it to be read. Let's look at a chart that summarizes key ideas about this topic.

Punctuation Mark	Used in a Sentence to Indicate a Pause or Break
Comma	After months of waiting, I finally downloaded the new album.
Dash	The new album—an amazing collection of songs—was exactly what I wanted.
Ellipsis	I finished listening to the album…and then listened to it again.

Figure 8.2.1 Examples of Punctuation Used to Indicate a Pause or Break

Grammatical Concept	What Is It?	What Are Some Punctuation Marks Used for this Purpose?	Why Is it Important?
Punctuation used to indicate a pause or break	Punctuation that writers use to show readers that they should briefly pause or break in a sentence while reading.	Comma (,) Dash (–) Ellipsis (…)	This concept is important to good writing because it helps readers understand what they're reading and allows them to read the work in the way the writer intended.

Figure 8.2.2 Key Information: Punctuation Used to Indicate a Pause or Break

Published Example of Comma Used to Indicate a Pause or Break	Published Example of a Dash Used to Indicate a Pause or Break	Published Example of an Ellipsis Used to Indicate a Pause or Break
"They didn't need to talk, which was perfect" (Emezi, 2019, p. 5). From *Pet* by Akwaeke Emezi	"But her good intentions are eclipsed by my anger and her betrayal–a dangerous combination" (Jean, 2022, p. 26). From *Tokyo Ever After* by Emiko Jean	"Are we going to…break up soon?" (Morris, 2022, p. 24). From *The Cost of Knowing* by Brittney Morris

Figure 8.2.3 Published Examples of Punctuation Used to Indicate a Pause or Break

I recommend displaying this chart while sharing its contents with students.

3. Mentor Text Example

In this part of the lesson, you'll share with students published examples of sentences in which writers use punctuation to indicate a pause or break, providing real-world examples of how this grammatical concept is used.

> We'll explore how punctuation that indicates a pause or break is used in published writing! We'll look together at three examples of punctuation used for this purpose. The first is from *Pet* by Akwaeke Emezi (2019) and contains an example of a comma used to indicate a pause or break. The second is from *Tokyo Ever After* by Emiko Jean (2022) and uses a dash for this purpose. The third is from *The Cost of Knowing* by Brittney Morris (2022) and features an ellipsis used for this reason.

I recommend displaying these mentor texts, reading them aloud, and identifying the punctuation used to indicate a pause or break in each one.

4. Mentor Text Discussion and Analysis Activities

You'll talk with students about the mentor texts and lead them through activities designed to help them understand the importance of the punctuation used to indicate a pause or break.

> We've seen published examples of punctuation used to indicate a pause or break. Now, we'll think about why that punctuation is important to the sentences in which it was used. We'll look at each of the mentor text sentences compared with revised versions that don't use the punctuation that indicates the pause or break in the sentence. Then, we'll reflect on how the punctuation impacts our experiences reading the passages. Let's start with the mentor text that uses commas to indicate a pause or break.

I suggest displaying these sentences and pointing out that one uses a comma to indicate a pause or break and the other does not.

> I'll ask you to discuss a reflection question about these sentences with a partner. The reflection question is 'How is your experience reading the sentence with a comma different from reading

Original Text	Revised Version that Doesn't Use a Comma to Indicate a Pause or Break
"They didn't need to talk, which was perfect" (Emezi, 2019, p. 5).	They didn't need to talk which was perfect.

Figure 8.2.4 Comma Mentor Text Compared with Revised Version

How Is Your Experience Reading the Sentence with a Comma Different from Reading the One that Does Not Contain a Comma?

Figure 8.2.5 Comma Reflection Question Graphic Organizer

140 ◆ Time for a Break: Punctuation that Indicates a Pause or Break

Original Text	Revised Version that Doesn't Use a Dash to Indicate a Pause or Break
"But her good intentions are eclipsed by my anger and her betrayal–a dangerous combination" (Jean, 2022, p. 26).	But her good intentions are eclipsed by my anger and her betrayal a dangerous combination.

Figure 8.2.6 Dash Mentor Text Compared with Revised Version

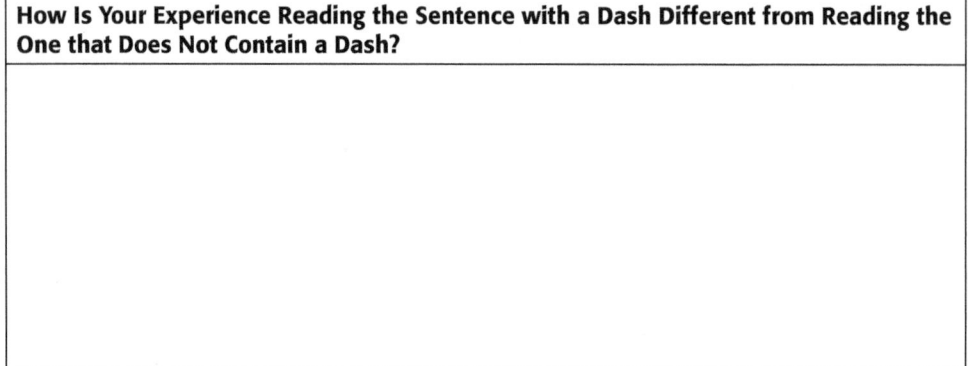

Figure 8.2.7 Dash Reflection Question Graphic Organizer

the one that does not contain a comma?' After you discuss, I'll ask for volunteers to share their ideas, which I'll record on a graphic organizer.

As students share their insights, I like to record them in this chart for the class to see.

Great job thinking about the importance of commas to that example. Let's analyze the importance of the dash to our mentor text that uses a dash to indicate a pause or break. I'll share with you that sentence compared with a revised version without the dash.

I recommend projecting these sentences and identifying where one uses a dash to indicate a pause or break and the other doesn't.

You'll talk with a partner about the following reflection question: 'How is your experience reading the sentence with a dash different from reading the sentence without the dash?' After you and your partner talk, volunteers will share and I'll record responses on a graphic organizer.

Original Text	Revised Version that Doesn't Use an Ellipsis to Indicate a Pause or Break
"Are we going to…break up soon?" (Morris, 2022, p. 24).	Are we going to break up soon?

Figure 8.2.8 Ellipsis Mentor Text Compared with Revised Version

How Is Your Experience Reading the Sentence with an Ellipsis Different from Reading the One that Does Not Contain an Ellipsis?

Figure 8.2.9 Ellipsis Reflection Question Graphic Organizer

When volunteers share, I recommend writing highlights of their responses on this chart.

> Good work thinking about the dash mentor text. Let's consider the significance of the ellipsis to our example that uses an ellipsis to indicate a pause or break. We'll look at that mentor text compared with a revised version with no ellipsis.

I like to display these examples and identify where one uses an ellipsis and the other does not.

> Let's think about a reflection question on these sentences. The question is 'How is your experience reading the sentence with an ellipsis different from reading the one that does not contain an ellipsis?' Please discuss this question with a partner. Afterwards, volunteers will share with the class; I'll record responses on a graphic organizer.

When students share, I write response highlights on this graphic organizer.

5. Exit Question

This lesson concludes with an exit question on using punctuation to indicate a pause or break.

"To conclude our work for today, you'll answer an exit question. Two volunteers will share answers out loud, and I'll collect everyone's answers. The exit question is 'Why would writers use punctuation to indicate a pause or break?'"

I suggest displaying this exit question and reading it aloud. When students turn in their answers, I use them to gauge their understandings of the topic.

Day Two
1. Introduction

To open the second day of instruction on punctuation that indicates a pause or break, you'll discuss with students how the day's activities we'll build on the previous day, share the key question for the day, and present the agenda.

> Great work yesterday on using punctuation to indicate a pause or break! You learned about this topic, examined published examples of it, reflected on the significance of that punctuation to the published examples, and answered an exit question about why writers use this concept. Today, we'll review important information about this topic, apply it to our writing, reflect on doing so, and answer an exit question about how using punctuation to indicate a pause can be important to our writing. Today's key questions are:
>
> ◆ How can we use punctuation to indicate a pause or break in our writing?
> ◆ How can using punctuation to indicate a pause or break impact our writing?
>
> Our agenda for today is:
>
> ◆ Review of using punctuation to indicate a pause or break
> ◆ Writing activity
> ◆ Reflection
> ◆ Exit question

I suggest displaying the key questions and agenda items as you share them with students.

What Does it Mean to Use Punctuation to Indicate a Pause or Break?	What Are Some Punctuation Marks Used for this Purpose?	Why Is Using Punctuation to Indicate a Pause or Break Important?	What Are Some Published Examples of Punctuation that Indicates a Pause or Break?
This is when writers use punctuation to show readers that they should briefly pause or break in a sentence while reading.	Comma (,) Dash (–) Ellipsis (…)	This concept is important to good writing because it helps readers understand what they're reading and allows them to read the work in the way the writer intended.	Published example using a comma: "They didn't need to talk, which was perfect" (Emezi, 2019, p. 5) Published example using a dash: "But her good intentions are eclipsed by my anger and her betrayal–a dangerous combination" (Jean, 2022, p. 26). Published example using an ellipsis: "Are we going to…break up soon?" (Morris, 2022, p. 24).

Figure 8.2.10 Review Information about Punctuation that Indicates a Pause or Break

2. Review of Using Punctuation to Indicate a Pause or Break

You'll provide students with a review of punctuation that indicates a pause or break, highlighting key information discussed in the previous class about this concept.

> We'll review important information about punctuation that indicates a pause or break by looking at a review chart. It contains information about what it means to use punctuation to indicate a pause or break, some punctuation marks used for this purpose, why this topic is important, and published examples of its use.

I recommend projecting this information and reading it aloud.

3. Writing Activity

Students use punctuation to indicate a pause or break in their writing, creating one sentence that uses a comma for this purpose, another that uses a dash, and a third that uses an ellipsis.

> Now that we've reviewed key information about using punctuation to indicate a pause or break, we'll apply this concept to our writing. You'll create three separate sentences: one will use a comma to

Example Sentence that Uses a Comma to Indicate a Pause or Break	Example Sentence that Uses a Dash to Indicate a Pause or Break	Example Sentence that Uses an Ellipsis to Indicate a Pause or Break
After we swam in the pool, we ate lunch.	We saw the waterslide—a huge structure next to the pool.	We slid down the waterslide… and then slid down it again.

Figure 8.2.11 Example Sentences for Writing Activity

> indicate a pause or break, one will use a dash, and one will use an ellipsis. Before you write, I'll share examples I created.

While you can use these sentences as examples with your students, I encourage you to create sentences of your own that you display for and share with students.

> "Now, you'll create three sentences of your own: one that uses a comma to indicate a pause or break, one that uses a dash, and one that uses an ellipsis."

When students compose their sentences, I move around the classroom to check on and support them.

> "Let's take two volunteers to share the sentences they created. When you share, please identify the type of punctuation you used to indicate the pause or break."

As volunteers share their work, I like to praise strong and effective uses of these punctuation forms to indicate a pause or break and provide any needed support.

4. Reflection

Students return to the sentences they created in the writing activity and reflect on the importance of using punctuation to indicate a pause or break in each of the sentences they created.

> We'll return to the sentences you just wrote and use them for a reflection activity. For each of the three sentences you wrote, you'll answer the question 'Why is the punctuation you used that indicates a pause or break important to the sentence?' You'll answer this question three times—once for each sentence.

I like displaying this question for students to read.

> Before you write, I'll share my reflections about my sentences. For the sentence 'After we swam in the pool, we ate lunch,' I wrote 'The comma is important because it tells readers to pause between 'pool' and 'we' and separates those parts of the sentence.' For the next sentence, 'We saw the waterslide—a huge structure next to the pool,'

I wrote 'The dash is important because it shows that readers should pause between 'waterslide' and the information describing it.' For the third one, 'We slid down the waterslide... and then slid down it again,' I wrote 'The ellipsis separates the two actions, shows readers they should pause between them, and builds suspense.'

I suggest reflecting on the importance of the punctuation that indicates a pause or break to the sentences you shared with students.

"Now, revisit the sentences you wrote and write a response to the question 'Why is the punctuation you used that indicates a pause or break important to the sentence?' for each sentence."

As students write, I circulate the classroom and support them with their responses.

"Let's take two volunteers to share their reflections. Afterwards, everyone will turn in their reflections and the sentences they wrote."

When students share, I recommend calling attention to strengths in their statements and providing any needed support.

5. Exit Question

This sequence concludes with an exit question on the importance of using punctuation to indicate a pause or break to students' writing.

We'll close with an exit question about punctuation that indicates a pause or break. You'll write your answers, two volunteers will share, and I'll collect the responses. The exit question is 'How can using punctuation to indicate a pause or break be important to your writing?'

I recommend displaying this question. When volunteers share responses, I suggest praising strong insights and providing any needed explanation.

Differentiation Suggestions

This lesson can differentiated in various ways:

- ◆ Students can explore additional mentor texts containing punctuation that indicates a pause or break.
- ◆ Students can examine mentor texts written on a range of reading levels.
- ◆ Students can create multiple example sentences.

Assessment

I recommend assessing students' knowledge of punctuation that indicates a pause or break in these ways:

- Students' exit question responses.
  - Students' answers to the exit questions in this instructional process provide useful assessment information regarding their understandings of punctuation that indicates a pause or break. When evaluating students' answers to the day-one exit question "Why would writers use punctuation to indicate a pause or break?," I assess how well they explain that writers use this type of punctuation intentionally to show readers when they should briefly pause or break when reading a sentence. When assessing students' answers to the day-two exit question "How can using punctuation to indicate a pause or break be important to your writing?," I evaluate how well students describe the importance of this concept and its potential role in their future writing.
- Students' written sentences and reflections.
  - The example sentences that students create containing punctuation that indicates a pause or break and the corresponding reflections can also be useful for assessment. I assess the sentences students create to determine if they used this type of punctuation correctly. I evaluate students' responses to gauge their awareness of the importance of this punctuation to the sentences they created.

Notes

- What worked when teaching this lesson?
- What might you adapt or change the next time you teach it?

References

Emezi, A. (2019). *Pet*. Knopf.
Jean, E. (2022). *Tokyo ever after*. Flatiron Books.
Morris, B. (2022). *The cost of knowing*. Simon & Schuster Books for Young Readers.

Lesson 8.3

Key Comparisons: Comparative and Superlative Degrees

Overview

This lesson focuses on the comparative and superlative degrees, forms of adjectives and adverbs used to express comparisons. There are two class periods in this sequence. On day one, students will learn what the comparative and superlative degrees are, examine examples of them, explore how they're used in published writing, and analyze those examples. On day two, students will review important information about the comparative and superlative degrees, use them in their writing, and reflect on the significance of using them in their works. At the conclusion of the process, students answer an exit question about why the comparative and superlative degrees are important to effective writing.

Objectives

- Students will understand the features of the comparative and superlative degrees.
- Students will learn the importance of the comparative and superlative degrees to effective writing.
- Students will use the comparative and superlative degrees in their writing and reflect on the importance of doing so.

DOI: 10.4324/9781003466826-17

Time Frame

Two class periods.

Background Knowledge Required

Students will need to be familiar with adjectives and adverbs.

Materials Needed

- Figures 8.3.1–8.3.6, which are displayed in the lesson plan, in Appendix B: Reproducible Graphic Organizers, and on the book's website.
- A projector, board, or piece of chart paper to display information.
- Paper for students' writing.

Detailed Plan

Day One
1. Introduction
To begin this instructional process, you'll introduce students to the comparative and superlative degrees, share the day's key questions, and provide the agenda.

> We're going to explore the comparative and superlative degrees, which writers use to make comparisons in their work. Today's big questions are:
>
> - What are the comparative and superlative degrees?
> - Why is using the comparative and superlative degrees important to writing?
>
> Here is our agenda for today:
>
> - Mini-lesson
> - Mentor text examples
> - Mentor text discussion and analysis activities
> - Exit question

I recommend displaying the questions and agenda items while reading them aloud.

2. Mini-Lesson

To conduct this mini-lesson on the comparative and superlative degrees, you'll explain what these concepts are, discuss important information about their usage, share examples of them, and talk about their importance to effective writing.

> In this mini-lesson, I'll introduce you to important information on the comparative and superlative degrees. Comparisons and superlatives are forms of adjectives and adverbs writers use to compare information. These degrees are important to writing because they help writers express comparisons and relationships in ways that readers can easily understand. We use comparative degrees to compare two things and superlative degrees to compare three or more things. For example, I would use the comparative degree to say 'Kate is faster than Jill.' In this sentence, 'faster' is in the comparative degree. I'd use the superlative to say 'Kate is the fastest runner on the team.' In that sentence, 'fastest' is in the superlative degree. Let's look at a chart with information about how to form the comparative and superlative degrees.

I suggest displaying this chart, reading its information for students, and discussing any questions they have. I like to keep this information displayed so that students can refer back to it.

Way the Comparative and Superlative Degrees Are Formed	Examples	Types of Words it Generally Applies To
Use "-er" ending for comparative and "-est" ending for superlative	Comparative: Faster Superlative: Fastest	◆ One-syllable adjectives ◆ One-syllable adverbs ◆ Two-syllable adjectives that end in -er, -ow, -le, and -y
Add "more" before the word for comparative and "most" before the word for superlative	Comparative: More talented Superlative: Most talented	◆ Two-syllable adjectives that do not end in -er, -ow, -le, and -y ◆ Two-syllable adverbs ◆ Three-syllable adjectives
Irregular formations	Comparative: Better Superlative: Best	Some words don't follow the typical structures and instead are formed in irregular ways. Some frequently used words with irregular comparative and superlative forms are good (comparative: better; superlative: best), bad (comparative: worse; superlative: worst), and many (comparative: more; superlative: most).

Figure 8.3.1 Information about Forming the Comparative and Superlative Degrees

Grammatical Concepts	Description	Ways They Can Be Formed	Why They Are Important to Good Writing
Comparative and superlative degrees	Comparative and superlative degrees are forms of adjectives and adverbs writers use to compare information. Writers use comparative degrees to compare two things and superlative degrees to compare three or more things.	Use "-er" ending for comparative and "-est" ending for superlative Add "more" before the word for comparative and "most" before the word for superlative Irregular formations	The comparative and superlative degrees are important to good writing because they help writers express comparisons and relationships in ways that readers can easily understand.

Figure 8.3.2 Comparative and Superlative Degree Key Information

Published Example of Comparative Degree	Published Example of Superlative Degree
"It was easier to imagine a world of possibilities, a world where literally anyone could be related to her" (Benway, 2017, p. 25). From *Far From the Tree* by Robin Benway	"Next to the city's numerous ruins, Elantine's golden tower was the oldest structure in the Empire" (Garber, 2018, p. 85). From *Legendary* by Stephanie Garber

Figure 8.3.3 Published Examples of the Comparative and Superlative Degrees

"Now, let's look at a chart that summarizes key ideas about the comparative and superlative degrees."

3. Mentor Text Examples

You'll share with students published examples of authors using the comparative and superlative degrees, providing authentic examples of how these concepts are used.

> Now, let's explore how published authors use the comparative and superlative degrees in their work. I'm going to share with you a published example of the comparative degree from the book *Far From the Tree* by Robin Benway (2017) and a published example of the superlative degree from the book *Legendary* by Stephanie Garber (2018).

I suggest displaying these sentences and reading them aloud. While reading them, I recommend pointing out the comparative degree example in the first sentence (the word "easier") and the superlative degree example (the word "oldest") in the second sentence.

4. Mentor Text Discussion and Analysis Activities

You'll lead students through activities designed to help them analyze the importance of using the comparative and superlative degrees to the respective published examples.

> Let's now think about the importance of the comparative and superlative degrees to the published examples that we just saw. First, we'll think about the comparative degree mentor text. I'll display that mentor text again along with an analysis question that asks us to think about why the use of the comparative degree is important to the sentence.

I recommend reading the mentor text and the analysis question aloud for students.

"Now, please talk with a partner about this analysis question. After you discuss the question with a partner, I'll ask for volunteers to share their responses with the class."

While students talk with their partners, I like to check in with them about their progress, praising strong responses and supporting students when needed. Strong responses will show students' awareness that the comparative degree is important because it helps the author express a comparison between two things in this passage. After students share with partners, I ask for volunteers to share with the class and record response highlights on the chart.

> Great work analyzing the comparative degree mentor text! Now, we'll do similar work with our superlative degree mentor text. I'll

Comparative Degree Mentor Text	Why Do You Think the Use of the Comparative Degree Is Important to the Sentence?
"It was easier to imagine a world of possibilities, a world where literally anyone could be related to her" (Benway, 2017, p. 25).	

Figure 8.3.4 Comparative Degree Mentor Text and Analysis Question

Superlative Degree Mentor Text	Why Do You Think the Use of the Superlative Degree Is Important to the Sentence?
"Next to the city's numerous ruins, Elantine's golden tower was the oldest structure in the Empire" (Garber, 2018, p. 85).	

Figure 8.3.5 Superlative Degree Mentor Text and Analysis Question

display the superlative degree example with an analysis question about why the use of the superlative degree is important to that sentence.

I suggest reading this mentor text and analysis question out loud for students.

"Just like you did with the last analysis question, please discuss this question with a partner. Afterward, volunteers will share responses with the class."

As students talk about this analysis question, I again circulate the classroom to provide praise and support. Strong answers will show students' understandings that the superlative degree is important to this sentence because it shows that the author is comparing three or more things and that this tower is the oldest of all of those things. Once students have completed sharing their answers with partners, volunteers share with the class while I record highlights on the chart.

5. Exit Question

The class period ends with an exit question on the comparative and superlative degrees.

You'll write an answer to an exit question about the comparative and superlative degrees. After you write, two volunteers will share answers out loud and then I'll collect everyone's work. The exit question is 'Why would writers use the comparative and superlative degrees?'

I recommend displaying this question while reading it aloud. I suggest reviewing the responses students turn in to evaluate their understandings of these concepts.

Day Two
1. Introduction
To begin the second day on the comparative and superlative degrees, you'll share with students how their work that day connects to the previous day's activities, discuss the day's key questions, and present the agenda.

> Great work on the comparative and superlative degrees yesterday! You learned important information about these concepts, read published examples of them, analyzed those examples, and answered an exit question about why writers would use these concepts. We'll explore the comparative and superlative degrees even further today. We'll review key information about them, use them in our writing, and reflect on the significance of using them. Finally, we'll answer an exit question about why these concepts are important tools for effective writing. Today's key questions are:
>
> ◆ How can we use the comparative and superlative degrees in our writing?
> ◆ Why is using the comparative and superlative degrees important to effective writing?
>
> Here is today's agenda:
>
> ◆ Review of comparative and superlative degrees
> ◆ Writing activity
> ◆ Reflection
> ◆ Exit question

I suggest displaying these questions and agenda items as you share the information with students.

2. Review of Comparative and Superlative Degrees
You'll review important information on the comparative and superlative degrees, addressing the description, formations, examples, and importance of these concepts discussed in the previous class.

> We'll review key information about the comparative and superlative degrees by looking together at a review chart about these topics.

What Are the Comparative and Superlative Degrees?	What Are Ways They Can Be Formed?	Why Are They Important to Good Writing?	What Are Some Published Examples of Them?
Comparative and superlative degrees are forms of adjectives and adverbs writers use to compare information. Writers use comparative degrees to compare two things and superlative degrees to compare three or more things.	Use "-er" ending for comparative and "-est" ending for superlative Add "more" before the word for comparative and "most" before the word for superlative Irregular formations	The comparative and superlative degrees are important to good writing because they help writers express comparisons and relationships in ways that readers can easily understand.	Published Example of Comparative Degree: "It was easier to imagine a world of possibilities, a world where literally anyone could be related to her" (Benway, 2017, p. 25). Published Example of Superlative Degree: "Next to the city's numerous ruins, Elantine's golden tower was the oldest structure in the Empire" (Garber, 2018, p. 85).

Figure 8.3.6 Comparative and Superlative Degree Review Information

This chart highlights information about what the comparative and superlative degrees are, ways they're formed, why they're important, and how they can look in published writing.

I recommend displaying this information, reading it aloud, and providing any additional explanation that could be helpful for students.

3. Writing Activity

Students apply the comparative and superlative degrees to their writing. They create a sentence using the comparative degree and another containing the superlative degree.

> We'll now use the comparative and superlative degrees in our writing! You'll write a sentence that uses the comparative degree to compare two things, and then you'll write another that uses the superlative degree to compare two or more things. An example comparative degree sentence I created is 'Joe is younger than Brian.' In this sentence, 'younger' is in the comparative degree. An example superlative degree sentence I wrote is 'Kevin is the youngest student in the class.' Here, 'youngest' is in the superlative degree.

I suggest creating your own examples of the comparative and superlative degrees, displaying them, and sharing them with students.

"It's your turn. Create a sentence that uses the comparative degree and another that uses the superlative degree. Please underline the comparative and superlative degree examples in the sentences. Once you're done, please share with a partner. Volunteers will share with the class."

While students write, I like to move around the room and support them as they use the comparative and superlative degrees.

"Now, share with a partner the sentences you created. Identity which one is in the comparative degree and which one is in the superlative degree."

When students share with partners, I again circulate the classroom, listening to what students share and providing support.

"Let's now have two volunteers share the comparative and superlative degree sentences they created and identify the comparative and superlative degree examples in those sentences."

During the time when students share, I recommend praising strong work and providing any explanations that can support students' understandings.

4. Reflection

Here, students revisit the sentences they created in the writing activity and reflect on why the comparative and superlative degrees are important to the sentences they wrote.

> We're going to return to the sentences you just created and use them for a writing activity. You'll revisit your comparative degree sentence and use it to answer the question 'Why is the comparative degree important to this sentence?' You'll then revisit your superlative degree sentence and use it to answer the question 'Why is the superlative degree important to this sentence?'

I like to display these questions for students.

> I'll share my reflections about the comparative and superlative degree sentences I created. For my comparative degree sentence 'Joe is younger than Brian,' I wrote 'The comparative degree is important to this sentence because it shows that two things are being compared—Joe and Brian's ages.' For my superlative degree sentence "Kevin is the youngest student in the class.' I wrote 'The superlative degree is important to this sentence because it shows that Kevin's age is being compared to the ages all of the students in the class.'

I suggest creating your own reflections about the comparative and superlative degree examples you created and sharing these reflections with students as examples.

Reread the comparative and superlative degree examples you created and write a response to this question for your comparative degree sentence: 'Why is the comparative degree important to this sentence?' Then, write an answer to this question for your superlative degree sentence 'Why is the superlative degree important to this sentence?'

As students write, I recommend checking in with them and providing any needed support.

"Now that you've written these reflections, talk with a partner and share your responses with them."

I like to move around the room and give feedback while students share with their partners.

"Let's have two volunteers share their reflection responses with the class. Then, everyone will turn in their reflections and their comparative and superlative degree sentences."

When volunteers share, I suggest noting strong reflections and providing any needed clarification.

5. Exit Question

This process concludes with an exit question on the importance of the comparative and superlative degrees.

Now, you'll answer an exit question on the comparative and superlative degrees. You'll write your answers, volunteers will share with the class, and I'll collect everyone's work. The exit question is 'Why are the comparative and superlative degrees important tools for effective writing?'

I recommend displaying this question while reading it aloud. When volunteers share, I suggest noting strong statements and adding any needed explanations.

Differentiation Suggestions

There are several ways to differentiate this lesson:

- ◆ Students can read comparative and superlative degree mentor texts on a variety of reading levels.
- ◆ Since the comparative and superlative degrees can take a number of forms, students can explore published mentor text examples of those forms.
- ◆ Students can write multiple passages containing the comparative and superlative degrees.

- Students can create examples of various comparative and superlative degree forms.

Assessment

I suggest assessing students' knowledge of comparative and superlative degrees in this instructional process in two ways:

- Students' exit question responses.
  - Students' exit question answers can tell a lot about their understandings of comparative and superlative degrees. When assessing students' responses to the first exit question, "Why would writers use the comparative and superlative degrees?," I evaluate how well they explain that writers use these concepts to compare information. When assessing students' answers to the second exit question, "Why are the comparative and superlative degrees important tools for effective writing?," I evaluate the detail and information students use when explaining that these concepts are important to good writing because they help writers clearly express comparisons and relationships for readers.
- Students' written passages and reflections.
  - The passages students write containing the comparative and superlative degrees and the reflections that align with those passages are excellent ways to assess students' knowledge. When evaluating students' passages, I assess if they correctly used the comparative and superlative degrees in ways that make sense for the piece. When assessing their reflections, I evaluate the information and detail they use when discussing why the comparative and superlative degrees are important to the sentences in which they were used.

Notes

- What worked when teaching this lesson?
- What might you adapt or change the next time you teach it?

References

Benway, R. (2017). *Far from the tree*. HarperTeen.
Garber, S. (2018). *Legendary*. Flatiron Books.

Lesson 8.4

Tools for Variety and Versatility: Using Verbals

Overview

This lesson focuses on verbals, grammatical concepts that are formed using verbs but do not function as verbs. On day one of this two-day lesson sequence, students will learn what verbals are, see examples of them, explore how these concepts are used in published writing, and consider their significance. On day two, students will review information about verbals, incorporate them in their writing, and reflect on the importance of using them. The instructional process concludes with students answering an exit question on how they can use verbals to maximize the effectiveness of their future writing.

Objectives

- Students will learn the characteristics of verbals.
- Students will understand the importance of verbals to strong writing.
- Students will use verbals in their writing and reflect on the significance of doing so.

Time Frame

Two class periods.

Background Knowledge Required

Students should be familiar with the concepts of verbs, adjectives, and adverbs.

Materials Needed

- Figures 8.4.1–8.4.10, which are available in the lesson plan, in Appendix B: Reproducible Graphic Organizers, and on the book's website.
- A projector, board, or piece of chart paper to display information.
- Paper for students to use when writing.

Detailed Plan

Day One
1. Introduction
To open this instructional process, you'll introduce students to the concept of verbals, share the key questions students will consider during that day's work, and provide the day's agenda.

> We're going to be exploring verbals, which are grammatical concepts that are formed using verbs, but do not function as verbs—they work as other parts of speech instead. As we'll explore in more detail, verbals provide writers with flexibility that helps them express information in clear and accurate ways. Today's big questions are:
>
> - What are verbals?
> - How can verbals be important to writing?
>
> Today's agenda is:
>
> - Mini-lesson
> - Mentor text examples
> - Mentor text discussion and analysis activities
> - Exit question

I recommend displaying the big questions and agenda items while reading them aloud.

2. Mini-Lesson

Now, you'll conduct a mini-lesson on the concept of verbals. To do so, you'll describe verbals, share examples of them, and discuss their importance to writing.

"In this mini-lesson, I'll introduce you to important information about verbals; this will be the foundation of the work we'll do on this topic. We'll start by talking about what verbals are: verbals are grammatical concepts that are formed using verbs but do not function as verbs. Instead, they work as other parts of speech instead. There are three kinds of verbals: gerunds, participles, and infinitives. Let's look at a chart that discusses each of these verbal types."

I suggest displaying this chart and discussing the descriptions and examples of the verbal types with students.

Verbals are important to writing because they provide writers with flexibility that helps them express information in clear and accurate ways. When writers use verbals, they can use verb forms as adjectives, adverbs, or nouns in their works—this gives writers a lot of ways to share information. Now, let's look at a chart that summarizes key information about verbals.

I recommend displaying this chart and reading its information aloud for students.

Kind of Verbal	Gerunds	Participles	Infinitives
Description	Gerunds are "-ing" forms of verbs that function as nouns. They can appear as single works or as gerund phrases, which are phrases that start with gerunds.	Participles are verb forms that function as adjectives. There are two kinds of participles: present participles (called the "-ing" form of a verb) and past participles (called the "-en" form of a verb). Like gerunds, participles can be used as single words or as phrases that begin with them.	Infinitives are formed by combining "to" with the base form of a verb, such as "to play." Like gerunds and participles, infinitives can be used as single words or to begin phrases. Infinitives can function as nouns, adjectives, or adverbs, depending on how they're used in a sentence.
Examples	**Swimming** is her favorite activity. ("Swimming" is a gerund.) **Swimming in the ocean** is her favorite activity. ("Swimming in the ocean" is a gerund phrase.)	**Waving**, they welcomed everyone to the party. ("Waving" is a present participle.) **Waving to the crowd**, they welcomed everyone to the party. ("Waving to the crowd" is a participial phrase that begins with a past participle.)	**To graduate** is her goal. ("To graduate" is an infinitive.) **To graduate from college** is her goal. ("To graduate from college" is an infinitive phrase.)

Figure 8.4.1 Kinds of Verbals

Grammatical Concept	What Are Verbals?	What Are Examples of Verbals?	Why Are Verbals Important to Writing?
Verbals	Verbals are grammatical concepts that are formed using verbs but function as other parts of speech, such as nouns, adjectives, or adverbs. The three kinds of verbals are gerunds, participles, and infinitives.	Gerund example: I enjoy **cooking**. Participle example: We met the **smiling** host. Infinitive example: They want **to win**.	Verbals are important to writing because they provide writers with flexibility that helps them express information in clear and accurate ways. When writers use verbals, they can use verb forms as adjectives, adverbs, or nouns.

Figure 8.4.2 Verbal Information

Published Gerund Example	Published Participle Example	Published Infinitive Example
"For a moment, I considered **hiding behind the wall** in the hopes that my aunt would mistake what she'd seen" (Rigaud, 2022, p. 5). From A Girl's Guide to Love and Magic by Debbie Rigaud **Hiding behind the wall** is a gerund phrase in this passage.	"The tracks push westward, the **setting** sun gilding the hillsides" (Sabic-El-Rayess, 2020, p. 3). From *The Cat I Never Named* by Amra Sabic-El-Rayess **Setting** is a participle in this passage.	"Maybe he doesn't want **to be a doctor**" (Yoon, 2016, p. 30). From The Sun Is Also A Star by Nicola Yoon **To be a doctor** is an infinitive phrase in this passage.

Figure 8.4.3 Published Examples of Verbals

3. Mentor Text Examples

In this part of the lesson, you'll share with students published examples of different types of verbals: gerunds, participles, and infinitives. This helps students see how these concepts are used in authentic situations.

"Let's take a look at how verbals are used in published writing. We'll examine published examples of three types of verbals: gerunds, participles, and infinitives. This chart contains examples of gerunds, participles, and infinitives used in published books."

I suggest displaying these sentences, reading them aloud, and identifying the verbal in each sentence.

4. Mentor Text Discussion and Analysis Activities

Here, you'll work with students to help them analyze the importance of the verbals to the published mentor texts they examined.

We've examined published examples of verbals. Now, we're going to think about and analyze the importance of the verbals

Gerund Mentor Text	Analysis Question: Why Is the Gerund Important to the Sentence?
"For a moment, I considered **hiding behind the wall** in the hopes that my aunt would mistake what she'd seen" (Rigaud, 2022, p. 5).	

Figure 8.4.4 Gerund Mentor Text and Analysis Question

Participle Mentor Text	Analysis Question: Why Is the Participle Important to the Sentence?
"The tracks push westward, the **setting** sun gilding the hillsides" (Sabic-El-Rayess, 2020, p. 3).	

Figure 8.4.5 Participle Mentor Text and Analysis Question

to each of those mentor text examples. First, we'll think about the published gerund example. I'll share with you a chart that contains the published example we previously saw and an analysis question.

I suggest reading this gerund mentor text for students and then reading the analysis question.

"Please talk with a partner about the analysis question. After you and your partner discuss, I'll ask for volunteers to share with the class. I'll record responses on this chart."

When students talk with partners, I suggest checking in with them about their progress, noting strong work and giving needed support. Strong responses will express that the gerund is important because it clearly expresses what the speaker considered. I then ask for volunteers to share with the class and record highlights on the chart.

"Great job analyzing the importance of that gerund. We'll now do similar work with the participle mentor text. I'll display the participle example with an analysis question about the importance of the participle."

Infinitive Mentor Text	Analysis Question: Why Is the Infinitive Important to the Sentence?
"Maybe he doesn't want **to be a doctor**" (Yoon, 2016, p. 30).	

Figure 8.4.6 Infinitive Mentor Text and Analysis Question

I recommend reading this participle mentor text and corresponding analysis question aloud.

"Now, talk with a partner about this analysis question. After you discuss with your partner, volunteers will share with the class."

While students talk together about the participle mentor text, I like checking with them and monitoring their progress. Strong responses will show students' understandings that the participle is important because it provides descriptive information about the sun. When students have finished sharing with partners, volunteers share with the class while I record highlights on the chart.

"Excellent work discussion the participle mentor text! We'll think now about the infinitive mentor text. I'll display the infinitive example along with an analysis question about why the infinitive is important to the sentence."
I suggest reading the gerund mentor text and analysis question aloud.

"Just like you did with the previous analysis questions, please discuss this question with a partner. Then, volunteers will share with the class."

As students discuss this analysis question, I again like to listen to their responses, providing praise and support. Strong responses will express that the infinitive is important because it clearly and accurately shows what the person doesn't want. Once students have finished sharing with partners, volunteers share with the class, and I write response highlights on the chart.

5. Exit Question

To conclude this class period, students answer an exit question on verbals.

"You'll write an answer to an exit question about verbals. After that, two volunteers will share responses aloud. I'll then collect everyone's written answers. The exit question is 'Why would writers use verbals in their works?'"

I suggest displaying this question while reading it out loud. After students turn in their responses, I like to review their answers to evaluate their understandings.

Day Two
1. Introduction
To open the second day of work on verbals, you'll let students know how the day's work will build on the previous day's activities, share the day's key questions, and present the agenda.

> Good job yesterday on our work with verbals! You learned important information about verbals, saw published examples of them, analyzed why the verbals in the published examples are important, and answered an exit question about why writers would use verbals. Today, we'll work even further on verbals. We'll first review key verbal information. Then, we'll use different types of verbals in our writing and reflect on the importance of using those verbals. We'll finish with an exit question about how you can use verbals in your future writing. Today's big questions are:
>
> ◆ How can we use verbals in our writing?
> ◆ How does the use of verbals impact our writing?
>
> Here's our agenda for today:
>
> ◆ Verbal review
> ◆ Writing activity
> ◆ Reflection
> ◆ Exit question

I suggest displaying the questions and agenda and reading it aloud for students.

2. Verbal Review
You'll review with students information about verbals, such as the attributes, importance, and examples of this topic discussed in the preceding class.

> We'll review key information about verbals. To do so, we'll look together at a review chart on this topic. The chart provides important information about what verbals are, shares examples, discusses why verbals are important, and displays the published mentor texts we saw in our last class.

What Are Verbals?	What Are Examples of Verbals?	Why Are Verbals Important to Writing?	What Are Published Examples of Verbals?
Verbals are grammatical concepts that are formed using verbs but function as other parts of speech, such as nouns, adjectives, or adverbs. The three kinds of verbals are gerunds, participles, and infinitives.	Gerund example: I enjoy **cooking**. Participle example: We met the **smiling** host. Infinitive example: They want **to win.**	Verbals are important to writing because they provide writers with flexibility that helps them express information in clear and accurate ways. When writers use verbals, they can use verb forms as adjectives, adverbs, or nouns.	Published Gerund Example: "For a moment, I considered **hiding behind the wall** in the hopes that my aunt would mistake what she'd seen" (Rigaud, 2022, p. 5). Published Participle Example: "The tracks push westward, the **setting** sun gilding the hillsides" (Sabic-El-Rayess, 2020, p. 3). Published Infinitive Example: "Maybe he doesn't want **to be a doctor**" (Yoon, 2016, p. 56).

Figure 8.4.7 Review Information about Verbals

Gerund Example	Participle Example	Infinitive Example
They love **dancing.**	We heard the **barking** dog.	I want to swim.

Figure 8.4.8 Verbal Examples

I recommend projecting this chart and reading aloud the information on it. This is also a great time to address any question or confusion students have about verbals.

3. Writing Activity

Here, students apply the concept of verbals to their writing by creating three sentences: one with a gerund, one with a participle, and one with an infinitive.

"We'll now apply our knowledge of verbals to our writing! You'll write three sentences: one that uses a gerund, one containing a participle, and one containing an infinitive. When you use these verbal types, you can use the verbal on its own or as part of a phrase. For example, you can use a gerund like 'running' or a phrase that starts with a gerund like 'running on the track.'"

"Before you start, I'll share some examples I created. This chart contains example sentences I wrote with each of the three verbal types."

I suggest creating your own sentences containing verbals, displaying them, and sharing them with students.

> It's time for you to create your own sentences containing verbals! Please create three sentences: one with a gerund, one with a participle, and one with an infinitive. Please underline the verbal you use. When you're done, you'll share your examples with a partner; volunteers will then share with the class.

While students write, I recommend circulating the classroom, checking on students' work, and providing support.

"Turn to a partner now and share what you wrote. Identify the verbals in your sentences."

When students share with partners, I move around the classroom, commenting on the examples they created.

"Let's have two volunteers share the sentences they created and identify the verbals in them."

As students share their verbal sentences, I praise strong usage of these concepts and clarify any misunderstandings.

4. Reflection

In this activity, students revisit the sentences they created and reflect on the importance of the verbals to each of those sentences.

> Now, we're going to use the sentences you just wrote in a reflective activity. You'll revisit the sentences you created and reflect on the importance of the verbals you used. This chart contains each of the three reflection questions you'll answer—there is one question for each verbal type.

I recommend displaying this chart and sharing the questions with students. You can also give this chart to students on paper or electronically so they can use it to answer their questions.

"Before you start, I'll share my answers to these reflection questions based on the sentences I wrote. I'll display a chart containing the sentences I created and my reflections."

I suggest creating reflections about the sentences you wrote containing verbals and sharing those reflections with students to provide models for their work.

"Please return to the sentences you wrote that contain verbals and answer these reflection questions for each one."

Reflection Questions	Why Is the Gerund You Used Important to the Sentence in Which You Used It?	Why Is the Participle You Used Important to the Sentence in Which You Used It?	Why Is the Infinitive You Used Important to the Sentence in Which You Used It?
Your Answers			

Figure 8.4.9 Reflection Questions

Reflection Questions	Why Is the Gerund You Used Important to the Sentence in Which You Used It?	Why Is the Participle You Used Important to the Sentence in Which You Used It?	Why Is the Infinitive You Used Important to the Sentence in Which You Used It?
Your Answers	The gerund "dancing" is important to the sentence "They love dancing" because it clearly expresses what they love doing.	The participle "barking" is important to the sentence "We heard the barking dog" because it provides descriptive information about the dog.	The infinitive "to swim" is important to the sentence "I want to swim" because it tells readers exactly what the speaker wants to do.

Figure 8.4.10 Reflection Question Answer Examples

While students write, I circulate the classroom to support their work and monitor their progress.

"Now, share your answers to the reflection questions with a partner; they'll then share their answers with you."

I recommend moving around the room while students share their responses with partners to listen to their reflections and provide feedback.

"We'll now have two volunteers share their reflections with the class. After that, everyone will turn in their reflections and their sentences that contain verbals."

When students share their reflections, I like to recognize strong statements and clarify information when needed.

5. Exit Question

At the conclusion of this instructional process, students answer an exit question about how they can use verbals in their future writing.

Now, you'll write an answer to an exit question about verbals. After you do, two volunteers will share their answers aloud. I'll then collect everyone's work. The exit question is 'How can you use verbals to maximize the effectiveness of your future writing?'

I suggest displaying the exit question while students write their answers. When volunteers share responses, I recommend identifying strong statements and providing any needed clarification or explanation.

Differentiation Suggestions

This lesson can be differentiated in several ways:

- Students can examine additional mentor texts containing verbals.
- Students can read mentor texts containing verbals written on various reading levels.
- Students can write additional sentences containing verbals.
- Students can use multiple verbals in individual sentences.

Assessment

I suggest assessing students' knowledge of verbals in this instructional process in two ways:

- Students' exit question responses.
  - Students' answers to the exit questions are useful for assessing their understandings of verbals. When evaluating students' answers to the day-one exit question "Why would writers use verbals in their

works?," I assess how well they explain that writers use verbals because verbals can help them express information in clear and accurate ways by using verb forms as other parts of speech. When assessing students' responses to the day-two exit question "How can you use verbals to maximize the effectiveness of your future writing?," I evaluate the clarity and detail students provide when explaining that they can use the flexibility that verbals provide to share ideas clearly and effectively with their readers.
- Students' written passages and reflections.
  - The sentences students create that use verbals and the corresponding reflections also provide useful assessment information. When evaluating students' sentences, I look to see if they used verbals accurately and if those verbals maximize the clarity of the sentence. When assessing their reflections, I gauge the information and detail they share when discussing the importance of each verbal.

Notes

- What worked when teaching this lesson?
- What might you adapt or change the next time you teach it?

References

Rigaud, D. (2022). *A girl's guide to love and magic*. Scholastic.
Sabic-El-Rayess, A. (2020). *The cat I never named*. Bloomsbury.
Yoon, N. (2016). *The sun is also a star*. Delacorte.

Lesson 8.5

The Many Moods: The Indicative, Imperative, Interrogative, Conditional, and Subjunctive Verb Moods

Overview

The lesson focuses on verb moods, which refers to what a verb expresses, such as a statement, a command, a question, a condition, or a desire. It addresses five verb moods: the indicative, imperative, interrogative, conditional, and subjunctive. On the first day of this two-lesson sequence, students will learn what the verb moods are, encounter examples of them, explore how verb moods are used in published writing, and consider their importance. On day two, students will review information about verb moods, apply the concept to their writing, and reflect on the importance of doing so. The sequence concludes with students answering an exit question about how the use of verb moods is important to their future writing.

Objectives

- Students will learn the characteristics of the verb moods.
- Students will understand the importance of the verb moods to effective writing.
- Students will use verb moods in their writing and reflect on the importance of doing so.

Time Frame

Two class periods.

Background Knowledge Required

Students should be familiar with the concept of verbs.

Materials Needed

- Figures 8.5.1–8.5.3. They are available in the lesson plan, in Appendix B: Reproducible Graphic Organizers, and on the book's website.
- A projector, board, or piece of chart paper for displaying information.
- Paper for students' writing.

Detailed Plan

Day One
1. Introduction
You'll open this instructional process by introducing students to the topic of verb moods, sharing the key questions students will consider that day, and presenting the day's agenda.

> We're going to explore the concept of verb moods, which refers to what a verb expresses, such as a statement, a command, a question, a possibility, or a desire. Our big questions for today are:
>
> - What are the verb moods?
> - Why are the verb moods important to writing?
>
> Here is today's agenda:
>
> - Mini-lesson
> - Mentor text examples

- Mentor text discussion and analysis activities
- Exit question

I recommend displaying these questions and agenda items while sharing them with students.

2. Mini-Lesson

You'll conduct a mini-lesson on important information about verb moods. To do so, you'll discuss what verb moods are, describe five types of verb moods, and discuss their importance to effective writing.

> We'll discuss important information about verb moods—this will be the foundation for our work on this topic. We'll continue to discuss these ideas as we explore the concept of verb moods.
>
> We'll start with information about what verb moods are. The term verb moods refers to what a verb expresses, such as a statement, a command, a question, a condition, or a desire. Sometimes, when we communicate, we'll make a statement, or tell someone to do something, or ask a question. When we do these things, we're using the concept of verb moods. We'll discuss five types of verb moods: indicative, imperative, interrogative, conditional, and subjunctive. Let's look at a chart that describes these moods and provides examples of each.

I recommend displaying this chart, reading its information aloud for students, and elaborating on any topics you think students might find challenging.

Verb Moods	**Descriptions**	**Examples**
Indicative	The indicative mood makes a statement.	This is my favorite song.
Imperative	The imperative mood makes a command.	Walk the dog.
Interrogative	The interrogative mood asks a question.	Did she read the book?
Conditional	The conditional mood is used when an action is dependent on something else. It shows the condition needed for something to happen.	If I finish my homework, I will go to the game.
Subjunctive	The subjunctive mood is used to express a wish or recommendation, or to describe something that is not reality. There are two main ways the subjunctive is used: (1) In a statement that makes a recommendation, and (2) In a statement describing something that is not reality.	1. I suggest that you read this book. 2. If I were a narwhal, I would have a majestic horn.

Figure 8.5.1 Verb Mood Information

These verb moods are important to effective writing because they provide writers with a variety of ways to express an action or state of being in a statement. By using these moods, writers can structure sentences in a variety of ways and use the verbs in their sentences to clearly express a message.

3. Mentor Text Examples

In this section, you'll show students published examples of each of the verb moods; this will convey to students how these concepts are used in authentic situations.

"Now, let's look at how the verb moods are used in published writing. I'm going to share with you a chart that contains published mentor text examples of each of the five verb moods we saw in our mini-lesson."

I recommend displaying this chart, reading the examples aloud, and talking with students about why each sentence is an example of the mood it represents.

4. Mentor Text Discussion and Analysis Activities

In this section of the instructional process, you'll divide students into five groups. They'll work in those groups to discuss and analyze the published mentor text examples of verb moods they encountered in the last activity.

We've seen published examples of five different verb moods. Now, we're going to work on analyzing the importance of each of those verb moods to the example in which they were used. I'm going to divide you into five groups, and I'll give each group one of the published mentor text examples we saw in our last activity. As a group, you'll discuss your verbal mentor text and create a response to this question:

Indicative Mood Example	Imperative Mood Example	Interrogative Mood Example	Conditional Mood Example	Subjunctive Mood Example
"The Sinclairs are athletic, tall, and handsome" (Lockhart, 2018, p. 3). From *We Were Liars* by E. Lockhart	"Help her!" (Collins, 2020, p. 188). From *The Ballad of Songbirds and Snakes* by Suzanne Collins	"How does this woman know my name?" (Colbert, 2019, p. 2). From *The Revolution of Birdie Randolph* by Brandy Colbert	"'Let's wait and see if the kid survives the beach landing,' Big John said. 'Then we can worry about a nickname for him'" (Gratz, 2018, p. 15). From *Grenade* by Alan Gratz	"If they knew anything about us, they'd know you can't perform in that" (Allen, 2023, p. 2). From *All You Have to Do* by Autumn Allen

Figure 8.5.2 Published Verb Mood Examples

Verb Mood	Mentor Text	Why the Verb Mood Is Important to the Example's Effectiveness
Indicative	"The Sinclairs are athletic, tall, and handsome" (Lockart, 2018, p. 3).	
Imperative	"Help her!" (Collins, 2020, p. 188).	
Interrogative	"How does this woman know my name?" (Colbert, 2019, p. 2).	
Conditional	"'Let's wait and see if the kid survives the beach landing,' Big John said. 'Then we can worry about a nickname for him'" (Gratz, 2018, p. 15).	
Subjunctive	"If they knew anything about us, they'd know you can't perform in that" (Allen, 2023, p. 2).	

Figure 8.5.3 Verb Mood Mentor Text Analysis Chart

'Why is the verb mood of your example important to its effectiveness?' When you discuss this question, I encourage you to think about the impact of the verb mood on the sentence, the benefits of the author using that mood, and how the mood helps the author deliver their message. I'm going to display the mentor text example chart we saw in our last activity. I'll then assign each group an example that they'll analyze by answering the analysis question. I'll come around and support you while you work. Once everyone is done with the discussion, each group will share highlights of its conversation with the class.

I recommend displaying Figure 8.5.2 and writing the analysis question "Why is the verb mood of your example important to its effectiveness?" on the board. While student groups work on their assigned sentences, I like to circulate, listen to their insights, and provide relevant praise and support. I listen for students' analyses of the impact the verb mood has on the piece, the benefits of its use, and how it helps the author deliver the message conveyed in the work. When the groups have finished their discussions, I call the class together to share.

"Great job discussing these ideas. Each group will share highlights of its conversation; I'll record information each group shares on this chart."

While student groups share their responses, I suggest praising especially strong analyses and providing additional elaboration and clarification when relevant.

5. Exit Question

This class period ends with an exit question on why writers would consider verb moods.

"To end today's work, you'll write an answer to an exit question on verb moods. Two volunteers will share responses verbally. I'll then collect everyone's responses. The exit question is 'Why would writers consider verb moods as they write?'"

I recommend displaying this question while reading it aloud. After students turn in their answers, I like to review their responses to gauge their understandings; this information can inform future instruction.

Day Two
1. Introduction

To begin the second class on verb moods, you'll talk with students about how their work will build on the previous day's, share the key questions, and present the day's agenda.

> Great work yesterday on verb moods! You learned key information about this topic, explored published examples of verb moods, analyzed the importance of those verb moods to the effectiveness of the published examples, and answered an exit question on why writers would consider verb moods. Today, we'll think even further about this concept. We'll start by reviewing key information about verb moods. Then, we'll apply this concept to our writing and reflect on the importance of doing so. We'll end with an exit question on how the use of verb moods is important to your future writing. Today's key questions are:
>
> ◆ How can we apply the concept of verb moods to our writing?
> ◆ How are the verb moods we use important to our writing?
>
> Our agenda for today is:
>
> ◆ Review of verb moods
> ◆ Writing activity
> ◆ Reflection
> ◆ Exit question

I suggest displaying the questions and agenda as you share this information with students.

2. Review of Verb Moods

In this section, you'll review key information about verb moods, such as their types, descriptions, examples, and importance discussed in the previous class.

"To get started, we'll review important information about verb moods. Let's go over the chart we looked at in yesterday's class that identifies five types of verb moods, descriptions of each one, and examples of each mood."

Here, you'll display Figure 8.5.1: Verb Mood Information again and read its verb moods, descriptions, and examples aloud while students follow along. If students have shown confusion about any of the verb moods, you can also use this time to discuss any confusion they have.

> In addition to reviewing verb mood types, descriptions, and examples, let's also review the importance of verb moods. Like we talked about yesterday, these verb moods are important to effective writing because they provide writers with a variety of ways to express an action or a state of being. By using these moods, writers can structure sentences in a variety of ways and use the verbs in their sentences to clearly express a message.

3. Writing Activity

In this activity, students create two sentences, with each sentence using a different verb mood.

> Now, we'll use verb moods in our writing! You'll write two sentences—each one will use a different verb mood. You can pick any of the five verb moods you would like to use for this activity as long as each of your two sentences uses a different mood. Before you write, I'll share the examples I created. I wrote a sentence in the indicative mood that reads 'The dog has thick fur.' I then wrote a sentence in the subjunctive mood that reads 'If I were a dog with thick fur, I would stay out of the hot sun.'

I recommend writing two of your own sentences, displaying them, and identifying their moods for students.

"Now, it's your turn! You'll create two sentences that represent different verb moods and identify the moods of those sentences. After you write, you'll share with a partner; volunteers will share with the class."

While students write, I suggest circulating the classroom to provide support as the students create their sentences.

"Good job creating your sentences. Share with a partner the sentences you created and the verb moods of those sentences."

As students share with partners, I like to again move around the classroom to hear what students share and provide any needed guidance.

"Now, let's have two volunteers share the sentences they wrote and the verb moods in those sentences."

When students share their verb mood examples, I recommend praising strong examples and identifications of those verb moods and giving any relevant explanation and clarification.

4. Reflection

Here, students revisit the sentences they created and reflect on the importance of the verb to the effectiveness of each sentence.

> We'll use the two verb mood example sentences you wrote in our last activity to reflect on the importance of verb moods. After you revisit your sentences, you'll answer this question for each sentence: 'Why is the verb mood in this sentence important to the effectiveness of the sentence?'

I like displaying this question for students while sharing it.

> Before you do this, I'll share my reflections about the sentences I wrote. For the indicative mood sentence 'The dog has thick fur,' I wrote 'The indicative verb mood is important to the effectiveness of this sentence because it clearly makes a statement about the dog's fur.' For the subjunctive mood sentence 'If I were a dog with thick fur, I would stay out of the hot sun,' I wrote 'The subjunctive mood is important to the effectiveness of this sentence because it clearly shows that I am describing a situation that is not reality. I'm not a dog with thick fur, and I can use the subjunctive mood to clearly express this.'

Now, it's your turn! You'll revisit your sentences and write an answer to the reflection question 'Why is the verb mood in this sentence important to the effectiveness of the sentence?' for each of the two sentences.

While students write, I suggest circulating to check on their progress and support their work.

"Good job working on those reflections. Share what you wrote with a partner and they'll do the same."

I recommend moving around the room while students share with their partners to provide support and praise strong insights.

"I'll now ask for two volunteers to share their reflections out loud with the class. Then, everyone will turn in their reflections along with the sentences they wrote for the writing activity."

> *When students share, I identify particularly strong reflections. I also provide clarification and further explanation if students have shown any misunderstandings.*

5. Exit Question
To conclude this instructional sequence, students answer an exit question on the importance of verb moods to their future writing.

> We'll wrap up our work with an exit question on verb moods. After you write your answers, I'll ask for two volunteers to share. I'll then collect everyone's papers. The exit question is 'How is the use of verb moods important to your future writing?'

I recommend displaying this exit question for students. When volunteers share responses, I suggest calling attention to strong points and sharing further explanation as needed.

Differentiation Suggestions

This lesson can be differentiated in numerous ways:

- Students can read additional mentor texts containing verb moods to give them additional exposure to how published authors use these concepts.
- Students can examine verbal mentor texts on a variety of reading levels.
- During the mentor text discussion and analysis activities, student groups can analyze multiple examples of a single verb mood or multiple types of verb moods.
- In the writing activity, students can create sentences that represent additional types of verb moods.

Assessment

I suggest assessing students' knowledge of verbals in two ways:

- Students' exit question responses.
  - Students' responses to their exit questions provide useful ways to assess their knowledge of verbals. When assessing students' answers to the first exit question, "Why would writers consider

verb moods as they write?," I evaluate how well they explain that writers would consider verb moods in their writing in order to structure sentences in ways that align with their message. When evaluating students' responses to the second exit question, "How is the use of verb moods important to your future writing?," I assess the information and detail students share when explaining how they will use verb moods in their future work to construct sentences in a variety of ways and align those sentences with the messages they want to express.
- Students' written examples and reflections.
  - The examples of verb moods that students create and their corresponding reflections are also excellent ways to evaluate students' understandings of this topic. When assessing students' written examples, I evaluate if they correctly created and identified verb mood examples. When evaluating their reflections, I assess the insight and detail they share when discussing why the verb mood in each sentence is important to the sentence's effectiveness.

Notes

- What worked when teaching this lesson?
- What might you adapt or change the next time you teach it?

References

Allen, A. (2023). *All you have to do.* Kokila.
Colbert, B. (2019). *The revolution of Birdie Randolph.* Little, Brown.
Collins, S. (2020). *The ballad of songbirds and snakes.* Scholastic.
Gratz, A. (2018). *Grenade.* Scholastic.
Lockhart, E. (2018). *We were liars.* Ember.

SECTION FOUR

Final Thoughts and Resources

Conclusion: Using This Book to Maximize Grammar Instruction

The lesson plans in this book are designed to help students think about grammatical concepts as important tools for effective writing. Instead of relying on worksheets or out-of-context activities, these lessons incorporate mentor texts, writing activities, and reflections to help students think deeply about the importance and uses of grammatical concepts. The lessons are designed to present grammar in the context of effective writing. By thinking about grammar this way, students can see the grammatical concepts they learn about as skills that they add to their repertoire of writing knowledge. When students write, they can draw on these skills and tools to make their works as strong as possible.

In this concluding chapter, I highlight four aspects of this book's lesson plans and share ideas about maximizing those lesson plan components. The ideas I highlight here are:

- Emphasize that grammatical concepts are tools for communication
- Use mentor texts to provide authentic examples of grammatical concepts in action
- Create opportunities for applications of grammatical concepts in student writing
- Focus on reflection to help students understand the importance of grammatical concepts

Let's look at each of these ideas in detail!

Emphasize That Grammatical Concepts Are Tools for Communication

A key component of the lesson plans discussed in this book is that grammatical concepts are important because they are tools for meaningful and effective communication. This principle is at the heart of all of the examples, discussions, and activities featured in this text. When talking about grammar with students, I address the "why" behind the teaching and learning of grammar, emphasizing that grammatical concepts are important because they help us communicate effectively. When putting the lesson plans in this book into action in your classroom, I recommend taking this same approach by calling attention to the significance of the grammatical concepts you are discussing. For example, if you are discussing intensive pronouns (which are discussed in Lesson 6.2), you can call attention to the fact that writers use these concepts to add extra emphasis to a statement. Similarly, if you are discussing strong verbs and specific nouns (concepts that are addressed in Lesson 7.3), you can emphasize that writers use these tools to express information clearly and precisely. No matter the concepts you are discussing with your students, emphasizing the importance of those concepts to effective communication can make grammar instruction meaningful and useful.

Use Mentor Texts to Provide Authentic Examples of Grammatical Concepts in Action

A central aspect of this book—and to research-based grammar instruction (Ruday, 2020)—is the use of mentor texts, published exemplars of a grammatical concept. By using the mentor texts in this book to provide your students with authentic examples of grammatical concepts in action, you'll maximize your students' experiences learning about grammar. Published mentor texts convey to students that grammatical concepts don't just exist on worksheets or in textbooks—they are part of our everyday lives. For example, students who are learning about prepositional phrases (a topic discussed in Lesson 7.1) can examine published examples of how authors use prepositional phrases to add detail to their work. Doing so would provide increased authenticity and relevance to students' work with that concept. By seeing real-world examples of grammatical concepts used in published texts, students can explore how these concepts are used in action in real-world situations. Mentor texts convey the authentic uses of grammatical concepts and can help deepen students' awareness of the importance of those concepts.

Create Opportunities for Applications of Grammatical Concepts in Student Writing

The lesson plans in this book also focus on the application of grammatical concepts to student writing. By creating opportunities for our students to apply the grammatical concepts they learn to their own writing, we can help students see these concepts as tools that make an impact on written work. This practice is consistent with this book's approach that grammatical concepts are important elements of effective communication. To help our students understand the importance of grammar to effective writing, we can construct in-class opportunities for them to apply the concepts they're studying to written works they create. For example, if students are learning about relative clauses (a topic discussed in Lesson 7.2), they can maximize their experiences learning about this concept by creating sentences that include relative clauses. By applying this grammatical concept to their writing, students can see firsthand the impact that it has on a written text. Also, when students incorporate the grammatical concepts they're learning about into their own written works, they take an even more active role in their learning. They utilize the knowledge they've gained about the features and importance of a grammatical concept and use it in a written text they create.

Focus on Reflection to Help Students Understand the Importance of Grammatical Concepts

Another essential feature of the lesson plans in this book is the emphasis on student reflection. When students reflect on the importance of grammatical concepts to the published mentor texts and to the examples that students create, they develop their abilities to think metacognitively about the importance of those concepts to writing. By engaging in this metacognitive reflection, students will consider the role of grammatical concepts to effective writing, a practice that can maximize their understandings of the importance of grammar from a writer's perspective (Cook, 2020; Ruday, 2020). For example, when students reflect on the importance of adverbs to a published text and to a work they create (as discussed in Lesson 6.1), they develop their awareness of the role of adverbs to effective communication and the reasons writers use this concept in their works. The reflective activities throughout these lessons—including the exit questions, which prompt students to reflect on key ideas—are designed to generate students deep awareness and understandings of the importance and impact of the featured grammatical concepts.

I am honored that you have chosen to use this book in your grammar instruction. These lessons combine research and practice; they are based on the principles of mentor text-based and metacognition-focused grammar instruction. Each plan uses published mentor texts, application, and reflection to deepen students' awareness of what grammatical concepts are, why they're important to effective writing, how to use them to maximize the effectiveness of their own works, and how incorporating them can enhance the quality of their own writing. Thank you for choosing to use these lessons in your classroom!

References

Cook, L. S. (2020). Students as their own best critics: A metacognitive approach to teaching grammar in context. *ATEG Journal, 29*, 14–25.

Ruday, S. (2020). *The middle school grammar toolkit: Using mentor texts to teach standards-based language and grammar in grades 6–8*. Routledge Eye On Education.

Appendix A
Annotated Bibliography of Mentor Texts

This annotated bibliography is designed to provide you with a quick reference guide to all of the mentor text examples used in this book. If you want to find one of the book's mentor text examples quickly, you can use this guide to find all of the published excerpts featured in the lesson plans. The guide is organized alphabetically by author's last name and each entry includes important details designed to help you use literature to teach these grammatical concepts. It contains the following information: (1) The titles and authors of the works of literature featured in this book, (2) A key grammatical concept found in each work, (3) An excerpt from that work, previously featured in one of the book's lesson plans, that demonstrates exactly how the author uses that grammatical concept.

Alexander, K. (2014). *The crossover.* Houghton Mifflin Harcourt.
Book Title: *The Crossover*
Author: Kwame Alexander
Key Grammatical Concept: Relative clauses
Excerpt: "He has one pair of Air Jordan sneakers for every month of the year including Air Jordan 1 Low Barack Obama Limited Editions, which he never wears" (p. 11).

Allen, A. (2023). *All you have to do.* Kokila.
Author: Autumn Allen
Book Title: *All You Have to Do*
Key Grammatical Concept: Verb mood
Excerpt: "If they knew anything about us, they'd know you can't perform in that" (p. 2).

Benway, R. (2017). *Far from the tree.* HarperTeen.
Book Title: *Far From the Tree*
Author: Robin Benway
Key Grammatical Concept: Comparative degree
Excerpt: "It was easier to imagine a world of possibilities, a world where literally anyone could be related to her" (p. 25).

Copyright material from Sean Ruday (2025), *Grammar Toolkit Lesson Plans for Middle School*, Routledge

Callender, K. (2020). *King and the dragonflies.* Scholastic Press.
Book Title: *King and the Dragonflies*
Author: Kacen Callender
Key Grammatical Concept: Prepositional phrases
Excerpt: "Cicadas make their noise, and the breeze whispers through the trees" (p. 153).

Cartaya, P. (2019). *Marcus Vega doesn't speak Spanish.* Penguin Random House.
Book Title: *Marcus Vega Doesn't Speak Spanish*
Author: Pablo Cartaya
Key Grammatical Concept: Punctuation that sets off additional information
Excerpt: "The rumors about me have gone from fantastical (Godzilla with a crew cut) to realistic (assistant principal)" (p. 2).

Cartaya, P. (2018). *The epic fail of Arturo Zamora.* Puffin Books.
Book Title: *The Epic Fail of Arturo Zamora*
Author: Pablo Cartaya
Key Grammatical Concept: Pronoun case
Excerpt: "I was excited for the start of summer" (p. 4).

Colbert, B. (2019). *The revolution of Birdie Randolph.* Little, Brown.
Book Title: *The Revolution of Birdie Randolph*
Author: Brandy Colbert
Key Grammatical Concept: Verb mood
Excerpt: "How does this woman know my name?" (p. 2).

Collins, S. (2020). The ballad of songbirds and snakes. Scholastic.
Book Title: *The Ballad of Songbirds and Snakes*
Author: Suzanne Collins
Key Grammatical Concept: Verb mood
Excerpt: "Help her!" (p. 188).

Crowder, M. (2022). *Mazie.* Viking Books for Young Readers.
Book Title: *Mazie*
Author: Melanie Crowder
Key Grammatical Concept: Compound sentence
Excerpt: "The diner's packed with families tonight, so the show should be a hoot" (p. 4).

DuPrau, J. (2003). *The city of Ember.* Yearling.
Book Title: *The City of Ember*

Author: Jeanne DuPrau
Key Grammatical Concept: Punctuation that sets off additional information
Excerpt: "It was a mystery in itself, whatever it was, and Lina was determined to solve it" (p. 96).

Emezi, A. (2019). *Pet*. Knopf.
Book Title: *Pet*
Author: Akwaeke Emezi
Key Grammatical Concept: Punctuation used to indicate a pause or break
Excerpt: "They didn't need to talk, which was perfect" (p. 5).

Erskine, K. (2012). *The absolute value of Mike*. Puffin Books.
Book Title: *The Absolute Value of Mike*
Author: Kathryn Erskine
Key Grammatical Concept: Connotation and denotation
Excerpt: "Moo nodded at an abandoned Exxon station" (p. 20).

Garber, S. (2018). *Legendary*. Flatiron Books.
Book Title: *Legendary*
Author: Stephanie Garber
Key Grammatical Concept: Superlative degree
Excerpt: "Next to the city's numerous ruins, Elantine's golden tower was the oldest structure in the Empire" (p. 85).

Gratz, A. (2018). *Grenade*. Scholastic.
Book Title: *Grenade*
Author: Alan Gratz
Key Grammatical Concept: Verb mood
Excerpt: "'Let's wait and see if the kid survives the beach landing,' Big John said. 'Then we can worry about a nickname for him'" (p. 15).

Gratz, A. (2017). *Refugee*. Scholastic.
Book Title: *Refugee*
Author: Alan Gratz
Key Grammatical Concept: Complex sentence
Excerpt: "When they got close to the ramp, Papa hunkered down behind the last of the crates" (p. 37).

Hiaasen, C. (2023). *Wrecker*. Alfred A. Knopf.
Book Title: *Wrecker*
Author: Carl Hiaasen

Key Grammatical Concept: Punctuation that sets off additional information
Excerpt: "He says he's too full for dessert, and–as casually as possible–excuses himself from the dinner table" (p. 183).

Hiranandani, V. (2018). *The night diary.* Kokila.
Book Title: *The Night Diary*
Author: Veera Hiranandani
Key Grammatical Concept: Simple sentence
Excerpt: "We woke up at a little before seven" (p. 1).

Jean, E. (2022). *Tokyo ever after.* Flatiron Books.
Book Title: *Tokyo Ever After*
Author: Emiko Jean
Key Grammatical Concept: Punctuation used to indicate a pause or break
Excerpt: "But her good intentions are eclipsed by my anger and her betrayal–a dangerous combination" (p. 26).

Khan, H. (2018). *Amina's voice.* Simon and Schuster.
Book Title: *Amina's Voice*
Author: Henna Khan
Key Grammatical Concept: Adjectives
Excerpt: "Her green eyes and tiny nose remind me of my next-door neighbor's bad-tempered cat, Smokey" (p. 4).

Le, L. (2021). *A pho love story.* Simon and Schuster.
Book Title: *A Pho Love Story*
Author: Loan Le
Key Grammatical Concept: Passive voice
Excerpt: "The article was written" (p. 348).

Lockhart, E. (2018). We were liars. Ember.
Book Title: *We Were Liars*
Author: E. Lockhart
Key Grammatical Concept: Verb mood
Excerpt: "The Sinclairs are athletic, tall, and handsome" (p. 3).

Moore, D. B. (2017). *The stars beneath our feet.* Knopf Books for Young Readers.
Book Title: *The Stars Beneath Our Feet*
Author: David Barclay Moore
Key Grammatical Concept: Adverbs
Excerpt: "As I flew back home, I suddenly realized how heavy the gifts were that I had just bought in that shop" (p. 4).

Morris, B. (2022). *The cost of knowing*. Simon & Schuster Books for Young Readers.
Book Title: *The Cost of Knowing*
Author: Brittney Morris
Key Grammatical Concept: Punctuation used to indicate a pause or break
Excerpt: "Are we going to…break up soon?" (p. 24).

Oh, A. (2021). XOXO. HarperTeen.
Book Title: *XOXO*
Author: Axie Oh
Key Grammatical Concept: Active voice
Excerpt: "I stuff the note deep into my pocket" (p. 6).

Rigaud, D. (2022). A girl's guide to love and magic. Scholastic.
Book Title: *A Girl's Guide to Love and Magic*
Author: Debbie Rigaud
Key Grammatical Concept: Verbals
Excerpt: "For a moment, I considered hiding behind the wall in the hopes that my aunt would mistake what she'd seen" (p. 5).

Saeed, A. (2022). *Omar rising*. Nancy Paulsen Books.
Book Title: *Omar Rising*
Author: Aisha Saeed
Key Grammatical Concept: Intensive pronouns
Excerpt: "When I was accepted to Ghalib, the headmaster had called me himself to tell me the news" (p. 211).

Sabic-El-Rayess, A. (2020). *The cat I never named*. Bloomsbury.
Book Title: *The Cat I Never Named*
Author: Amra Sabic-El-Rayess
Key Grammatical Concept: Verbals
Excerpt: "The tracks push westward, the setting sun gilding the hillsides" (p. 3).

Thomas, A. (2023). Nic Blake and the Remarkables: The Manifestor Prophecy. Balzer + Bray.
Book Title: *Nic Blake and the Remarkables: The Manifestor Prophecy*
Author: Angie Thomas
Key Grammatical Concept: Prepositional phrases
Excerpt: "I tiptoe through the woods so the leaves don't crackle under my feet" (p. 2).

Venkatraman, P. (2019). *The bridge home.* Puffin Books.
Book Title: *The Bridge Home*
Author: Padma Venkatraman
Key Grammatical Concept: Pronoun case
Excerpt: "Homesickness pinched my heart for a moment" (p. 22).

Warga, J. (2021). *Other words for home.* Balzer + Bray.
Book Title: *Other Words for Home*
Author: Jasmine Warga
Key Grammatical Concept: Specific Nouns
Excerpt: "I asked him about the big skyscrapers…" (p. 3).

Watson, R. (2019). *Some places more than others.* Bloomsbury Children's Books.
Book Title: *Some Places More than Others*
Author: Renée Watson
Key Grammatical Concept: Adjectives
Excerpt: "I reach for the basket of homemade dinner rolls and pass it" (p. 6).

Williams, A. (2019). *Genesis begins again.* Atheneum Books for Young Readers.
Book Title: *Genesis Begins Again*
Author: Alicia D. Williams
Key Grammatical Concept: Strong Verbs
Excerpt: "Mama rummages through her dresser drawer" (p. 8).

Woodson, J. (2010). *Miracle's boys.* Nancy Paulsen Books.
Book Title: *Miracle's Boys*
Author: Jacqueline Woodson
Key Grammatical Concept: Pronoun case
Excerpt: "Newcharlie wasn't talking to me" (p. 2).

Yoon, N. (2016). *The sun is also a star.* Delacorte.
Book Title: *The Sun is Also a Star*
Author: Nicola Yoon
Key Grammatical Concept: Verbals
Excerpt: "Maybe he doesn't want to be a doctor" (p. 30).

Appendix B
Reproducible Graphic Organizers

This resource contains all of the graphic organizers featured in the book's lesson plans. The graphic organizers are grouped by their corresponding lesson plans for clarity and convenient access. These graphic organizers can also be downloaded from the Routledge website.

Graphic Organizers from Lesson 6.1: The Case of Communication: Pronoun Case

Pronoun Case	How It's Used	Examples	Example Used in a Sentence	Why It's Important
Subjective Case	We use the subjective case when referring to the subject of a statement.	I, We, You, He, She, It, They	**She** is playing in the game.	Subjective case pronouns clearly communicate to readers that they represent the subject of a statement without repeating the noun.

Figure 6.1.1 Subjective Case Pronoun Information

Copyright material from Sean Ruday (2025), *Grammar Toolkit Lesson Plans for Middle School*, Routledge

Pronoun Case	How It's Used	Examples	Example Used in a Sentence	Why It's Important
Objective Case	We use the objective case when referring to something that is in the "object" role in a statement, such as a direct object, indirect object, or object of a preposition.	Me, Us, You, Him, Her, It, Them	The dog saw **him**.	Objective case pronouns clearly communicate to readers that they represent a noun that is the "object" of something without repeating the noun.

Figure 6.1.2 Objective Case Pronoun Information

Pronoun Case	How It's Used	Examples	Examples Used in a Sentence	Why It's Important
Possessive Case	We use possessive case pronouns to show possession while taking the place of nouns.	My, Mine, Our, Ours, Your, Yours, His, Her, Hers, Its, Their, Theirs	That is **her** ball. That is **hers**.	Possessive case pronouns are important because of the ways they help us show possession in a piece of writing without repeating a person's name.

Figure 6.1.3 Possessive Case Pronoun Information

Published Example of Subjective Case	Published Example of Objective Case	Published Example of Possessive Case
"**I** was excited for the start of summer" (Cartaya, 2018, p. 4). From *The Epic Fail of Arturo Zamora* by Pablo Cartaya	"Newcharlie wasn't talking to **me**" (Woodson, 2010, p. 2). From *Miracle's Boys* by Jacqueline Woodson	"Homesickness pinched **my** heart for a moment" (Venkatraman, 2019, p. 22). From *The Bridge Home* by Padma Venkatraman

Figure 6.1.4 Published Examples of Pronoun Cases

Copyright material from Sean Ruday (2025), *Grammar Toolkit Lesson Plans for Middle School*, Routledge

Appendix B: Reproducible Graphic Organizers ◆ 195

Subjective Case Pronoun Mentor Text	Why the Subjective Case Pronoun Is Important to the Text
"**I** was excited for the start of summer" (Cartaya, 2018, p. 4).	

Figure 6.1.5 Subjective Case Pronoun Mentor Text Discussion Chart

Objective Case Pronoun Mentor Text	Why the Objective Case Pronoun Is Important to the Text
"Newcharlie wasn't talking to **me**" (Woodson, 2010, p. 2).	

Figure 6.1.6 Objective Case Pronoun Mentor Text Discussion Chart

Possessive Case Pronoun Mentor Text	Why the Objective Case Pronoun Is Important to the Text
"Homesickness pinched **my** heart for a moment" (Venkatraman, 2019, p. 22).	

Figure 6.1.7 Possessive Case Pronoun Mentor Text Discussion Chart

Copyright material from Sean Ruday (2025), *Grammar Toolkit Lesson Plans for Middle School*, Routledge

Graphic Organizers from Lesson 6.2: Bringing the Intensity: Intensive Pronouns

Grammatical Concept	What Are Intensive Pronouns?	What Are Examples of Intensive Pronouns?	How Can Intensive Pronouns Look in Writing?	Why Are Intensive Pronouns Important?
Intensive pronouns	Intensive pronouns are pronouns that end with 'self' or 'selves' and are used to add extra emphasis to a statement.	The words himself, herself, myself, yourself, yourselves, itself, themself, themselves, and ourselves are all intensive pronouns.	The mayor **herself** came to visit our school. I met the author **himself**!	Intensive pronouns are important to effective writing because they are a way for writers to add extra emphasis to a statement.

Figure 6.2.1 Intensive Pronoun Information

Original Text Containing Intensive Pronoun	Revised Version with Intensive Pronoun Removed
"When I was accepted to Ghalib, the headmaster had called me himself to tell me the news" (Saeed, 2022, p. 211).	When I was accepted to Ghalib, the headmaster had called me to tell me the news.

Figure 6.2.2 Original Text Containing Intensive Pronoun vs. Revised Version with Intensive Pronoun Removed

Reflection Question One	Reflection Question Two
How is the passage different without the intensive pronoun 'himself?'	Why do you think the author chose to use an intensive pronoun in this sentence?

Figure 6.2.3 Intensive Pronoun Reflection Questions Graphic Organizer

Copyright material from Sean Ruday (2025), *Grammar Toolkit Lesson Plans for Middle School*, Routledge

What Are Intensive Pronouns?	What Are Some Examples of Intensive Pronouns?	Why Are Intensive Pronouns Important?	What Is a Published Example of Intensive Pronoun Use?
Intensive pronouns are pronouns that end with 'self' or 'selves' and are used to add extra emphasis to a statement.	The words himself, herself, myself, yourself, yourselves, itself, themself, themselves, and ourselves are all intensive pronouns.	Intensive pronouns are important to effective writing because they are a way for writers to add extra emphasis to a statement.	"When I was accepted to Ghalib, the headmaster had called me himself to tell me the news" from the book *Omar Rising* (Saeed, 2022, p. 211).

Figure 6.2.4 Intensive Pronouns Review Information

Graphic Organizers from Lesson 6.3: Adding and Clarifying: Punctuation that Sets Off Additional Information

Grammatical Concept	What Is It?	What Are Some Examples Used in Sentences?	What Is It Important?
Punctuation That Sets Off Additional Information	Punctuation, such as commas, parentheses, and dashes, that is used to separate additional information from the main part of a sentence.	Newton, my amazing dog, greeted me at the door. Newton (my amazing dog) greeted me at the door. Newton—my amazing dog—greeted me at the door.	This concept is important because it identifies extra information for the reader.

Figure 6.3.1 Information about Punctuation That Sets Off Additional Information

Published Example Using Commas	Published Examples Using Parentheses	Published Example Using Dashes
"It was a mystery in itself, whatever it was, and Lina was determined to solve it" (DuPrau, 2003, p. 96). From *The City of Ember* by Jeanne DuPrau	"The rumors about me have gone from fantastical (Godzilla with a crew cut) to realistic (assistant principal)" (Cartaya, 2019, p. 2). From *Marcus Vega Doesn't Speak Spanish* by Pablo Cartaya	"He says he's too full for dessert, and—as casually as possible—excuses himself from the dinner table" (Hiaasen, 2023, p. 183). From *Wrecker* by Carl Hiaasen

Figure 6.3.2 Published Examples of Punctuation That Sets Off Additional Information

Copyright material from Sean Ruday (2025), *Grammar Toolkit Lesson Plans for Middle School*, Routledge

Mentor Text Example	Example Without Commas That Set Off Additional Information	Why the Commas Are Important to the Text
"It was a mystery in itself, whatever it was, and Lina was determined to solve it" (DuPrau, 2003, p. 96).	It was a mystery in itself whatever it was and Lina was determined to solve it.	

Figure 6.3.3 Mentor Text Discussion Chart: Commas That Set Off Additional Information

Mentor Text Example	Example Without Parentheses That Set Off Additional Information	Why the Parentheses Are Important to the Text
"The rumors about me have gone from fantastical (Godzilla with a crew cut) to realistic (assistant principal)" (Cartaya, 2019, p. 2).	The rumors about me have gone from fantastical Godzilla with a crew cut to realistic assistant principal.	

Figure 6.3.4 Mentor Text Discussion Chart: Parentheses That Set Off Additional Information

Mentor Text Example	Example Without Dashes That Set Off Additional Information	Why the Dashes Are Important to the Text
"He says he's too full for dessert, and–as casually as possible–excuses himself from the dinner table" (Hiaasen, 2023, p. 183).	He says he's too full for dessert, and as casually as possible excuses himself from the dinner table.	

Figure 6.3.5 Mentor Text Discussion Chart: Dashes That Set Off Additional Information

Graphic Organizers from Lesson 6.4: Developing and Describing: Adjectives

Grammatical Concept	What Are Adjectives?	What Are Some Examples of Adjectives?	What Are Some Ways Adjectives Can Look in Writing?	Why Are Adjectives Important?
Adjectives	Adjectives are descriptive words that provide information about a noun or pronoun.	Some examples of adjectives are young, old, warm, frigid, green, beautiful, unique, huge, majestic, fast, and enjoyable.	We saw the **majestic** lion. The **fast** player sprinted down the field. They enjoyed the **warm** day.	Adjectives are important to effective writing because they help the reader understand the characteristics of the noun or pronoun being described.

Figure 6.4.1 Adjective Information

Original Text Containing Adjectives	Revised Version with Adjectives Removed
"Her green eyes and tiny nose remind me of my next-door neighbor's bad-tempered cat, Smokey" (Khan, 2018, p. 4).	Her eyes and nose remind me of my neighbor's cat, Smokey.

Figure 6.4.2 Original Text Containing Adjectives vs. Revised Version with Adjectives Removed

Reflection Question One	Reflection Question Two
How is the sentence different without the adjectives?	Why do you think the author used the adjectives in the sentence?

Figure 6.4.3 Adjective Reflection Questions Graphic Organizer

Copyright material from Sean Ruday (2025), *Grammar Toolkit Lesson Plans for Middle School*, Routledge

What Are Adjectives?	What Are Some Examples of Adjectives?	Why Are Adjectives Important?	What Is a Published Example of Adjective Use?
Adjectives are descriptive words that provide information about a noun or pronoun.	Some examples of adjectives are young, old, warm, frigid, green, beautiful, unique, huge, majestic, fast, and enjoyable.	Adjectives are important to effective writing because they help the reader understand the characteristics of the noun or pronoun being described.	"Her **green** eyes and **tiny** nose remind me of my **next-door** neighbor's **bad-tempered** cat, Smokey" (Khan, 2018, p. 4).

Figure 6.4.4 Adjective Review Information

Graphic Organizers from Lesson 6.5: Explanation and Impact: Adverbs

Grammatical Concept	What Are Adverbs?	What Are Some Examples of Adverbs?	What Are Some Ways Adverbs Can Look in Writing?	Why Are Adverbs Important?
Adverbs	Adverbs are words that describe verbs, adjectives, and other adverbs, answering questions such as "How?," "When?," "Where?," and "To what extent?"	Some examples of words that can function as adverbs are quickly, slowly, skillfully, carefully, extremely, soon, often, frequently, immediately, happily, everywhere, exactly, truly, very, and sincerely.	The player **skillfully** kicked the ball. They spoke truly and sincerely. He looked everywhere. We **soon** learned the information. The team played **very** well.	Adverbs are important tools for effective writing because the explanation they provide can enhance a reader's understanding of the piece.

Figure 6.5.1 Adverb Information

Original Text Containing an Adverb	Revised Version with Adverb Removed
"As I flew back home, I suddenly realized how heavy the gifts were that I had just bought in that shop" (Moore, 2017, p. 4).	As I flew back home, I realized how heavy the gifts were that I had just bought in that shop.

Figure 6.5.2 Original Text Containing an Adverb vs. Version with Adverb Removed

Copyright material from Sean Ruday (2025), *Grammar Toolkit Lesson Plans for Middle School*, Routledge

Reflection Question One	Reflection Question Two
How is the sentence different without the adverb "suddenly"?	Why do you think the author used this adverb in the sentence?

Figure 6.5.3 Adverb Reflection Questions Graphic Organizer

What Are Adverbs?	What Are Some Examples of Adverbs?	Why Are Adverbs Important?	What Is a Published Example of Adverb Use?
Adverbs are words that describe verbs, adjectives, and other adverbs, answering questions such as "How?," "When?," "Where?," and "To what extent?"	Some examples of words that can function as adverbs are quickly, slowly, skillfully, carefully, extremely, soon, often, frequently, immediately, happily, everywhere, exactly, truly, very, and sincerely.	Adverbs are important tools for effective writing because the explanation they provide can enhance a reader's understanding of the piece.	"As I flew back home, I **suddenly** realized how heavy the gifts were that I had just brought in that shop" (Moore, 2017, p. 4).

Figure 6.5.4 Adverb Review Information

Graphic Organizers from Lesson 7.1: Developing Ideas: Prepositional Phrases

At	During
Above	In
Across	On
Before	Through
Down	Under

Figure 7.1.1 Some High-Frequency-Prepositions

Grammatical Concept	What Are Prepositional Phrases?	What Are Examples of Prepositional Phrases?	How Can Prepositional Phrases Look in Writing?	Why Are Prepositional Phrases Important?
Prepositional phrases	Prepositional phrases are descriptive phrases that begin with a preposition and end with a noun or pronoun called the object of the preposition.	On the field Before the game Above the clouds During the party	The players ran **on the field**. We ate before the game. The plane flew above the clouds. **During the party**, we celebrated.	Prepositional phrases are important because of the detail and description they add to a statement. This information can enhance the reader's understanding.

Figure 7.1.2 Prepositional Phrase Information

Original Text Containing Prepositional Phrase	Revised Version without Prepositional Phrase
"Cicadas make their noise, and the breeze whispers through the trees" (Callender, 2020, p. 153).	Cicadas make their noise, and the breeze whispers.

Figure 7.1.3 Original Text vs. Revised Version without Prepositional Phrase

Copyright material from Sean Ruday (2025), *Grammar Toolkit Lesson Plans for Middle School*, Routledge

Reflection Question One	Reflection Question Two
How is the sentence different without the prepositional phrase "through the trees"?	Why do you think the author used this prepositional phrase?

Figure 7.1.4 Prepositional Phrase Reflection Questions Graphic Organizer

What Are Prepositional Phrases?	What Are Some Examples of Prepositional Phrases?	Why Are Prepositional Phrases Important?	What Is a Published Example of Prepositional Phrase Use?
Prepositional phrases are descriptive phrases that begin with a preposition and end with a noun or pronoun called the object of the preposition.	On the field Before the game Above the clouds During the party	Prepositional phrases are important because of the detail and description they add to a statement. This information can enhance the reader's understanding.	"Cicadas make their noise, and the breeze whispers **through the trees**" (Callender, 2020, p. 153).

Figure 7.1.5 Prepositional Phrase Review Information

Copyright material from Sean Ruday (2025), *Grammar Toolkit Lesson Plans for Middle School*, Routledge

Graphic Organizers from Lesson 7.2: A Descriptive Tool: Relative Clauses

Relative Pronouns	Relative Adverbs
Who, Whose, Whom, Which, That	Where, When, Why

Figure 7.2.1 Relative Pronouns and Relative Adverbs

Grammatical Concept	What Are Relative Clauses?	What Are Examples of Relative Clauses?	How Can Relative Clauses Look in Writing?	Why Are Relative Clauses Important?
Relative clauses	Relative clauses are grammatical concepts that describe nouns and pronouns and begin with relative pronouns or relative adverbs.	who is a great soccer player when the soccer game starts which is her favorite food	Sam, **who is a great soccer player**, is playing today. I'm excited for 4:00pm, **when the soccer game starts.** After the game, Sam will eat pizza, **which is her favorite food.**	Relative clauses are important because they add descriptive information to a piece of writing. The description they provide can enhance the reader's understanding of the noun or pronoun being discussed.

Figure 7.2.2 Relative Clause Information

Original Text Containing Relative Clause	Revised Version Without Relative Clause
"He has one pair of Air Jordan sneakers for every month of the year including Air Jordan 1 Low Barack Obama Limited Editions, which he never wears" (Alexander, 2014, p. 11).	He has one pair of Air Jordan sneakers for every month of the year including Air Jordan 1 Low Barack Obama Limited Editions.

Figure 7.2.3 Original Text vs. Revised Version Without Relative Clause

Reflection Question One	Reflection Question Two
How is the sentence different without the relative clause "which he never wears"?	Why do you think the author used this relative clause?

Figure 7.2.4 Relative Clause Reflection Questions Graphic Organizer

What Are Relative Clauses?	What Are Some Examples of Relative Clauses?	Why Are Relative Clauses Important?	What Is a Published Example of Relative Clause Use?
Relative clauses are grammatical concepts that describe nouns and pronouns and begin with relative pronouns or relative adverbs.	who is a great soccer player when the soccer game starts which is her favorite food	Relative clauses are important because they add descriptive information to a piece of writing. The description they provide can enhance the reader's understanding of the noun or pronoun being discussed.	"He has one pair of Air Jordan sneakers for every month of the year including Air Jordan 1 Low Barack Obama Limited Editions, **which he never wears**" (Alexander, 2014, p. 11).

Figure 7.2.5 Relative Clause Review Information

Copyright material from Sean Ruday (2025), *Grammar Toolkit Lesson Plans for Middle School*, Routledge

Graphic Organizers from Lesson 7.3: Strong and Specific: Strong Verbs and Specific Nouns

Strong Verb	Weaker Verb Comparison
Sprinted	Went
Shouted	Said
Devoured	Ate

Figure 7.3.1 Strong Verbs Compared with Weaker Verbs

Specific Noun	General Noun Comparison
Hockey	Sport
Pizza	Food
Hawk	Bird

Figure 7.3.2 Specific Nouns Compared with General Nouns

Grammatical Concepts	What Are Strong Verbs and Specific Nouns?	What Are Examples of Strong Verbs and Specific Nouns?	How Can Strong Verbs and Specific Nouns Look in Writing?	Why Are Strong Verbs and Specific Nouns Important?
Strong verbs and specific nouns	Strong verbs express actions in ways that readers can easily understand. Specific nouns are nouns that are concrete, clear, and easy for readers to visualize.	Strong Verb Examples: Sprinted Shouted Devoured Specific Noun Examples: Hockey Pizza Hawk	Strong Verb in Writing: The players **sprinted** onto the field. Specific Noun in Writing: We are excited to get home and eat **pizza**.	Strong verbs and specific nouns are important because they allow writers to express information clearly and precisely. Without them, writing would be more general and harder to understand.

Figure 7.3.3 Strong Verb and Specific Noun Information

Published Example of Strong Verb	Published Example of Specific Noun
"Mama **rummages** through her dresser drawer" (Williams, 2019, p. 8). From *Genesis Begins Again* by Alicia D. Williams	"I asked him about the big **skyscrapers**..." (Warga, 2021, p. 3). From *Other Words for Home* by Jasmine Warga

Figure 7.3.4 Published Examples of Strong Verbs and Specific Nouns

Copyright material from Sean Ruday (2025), *Grammar Toolkit Lesson Plans for Middle School*, Routledge

Appendix B: Reproducible Graphic Organizers ◆ 207

Strong Verb Mentor Text	Revised Version with Strong Verb Replaced by Weaker Verb	Specific Noun Mentor Text	Revised Version with Specific Noun Replaced by General Noun
"Mama **rummages** through her dresser drawer" (Williams, 2019, p. 8).	Mama **looks** through her dresser drawer.	"I asked him about the big **skyscrapers**…" (Warga, 2021, p. 3).	I asked him about the big **buildings**.

Figure 7.3.5 Strong Verb and Specific Noun Mentor Texts Compared with Revised Versions

Reflection Question One	Reflection Question Two
How is the sentence with a strong verb different from the one with a weaker verb?	How is the sentence with a specific noun different from the one with a general noun?

Figure 7.3.6 Strong Verb and Specific Noun Reflection Graphic Organizer

What Are Strong Verbs and Specific Nouns?	What Are Some Examples of Strong Verbs and Specific Nouns?	Why Are Strong Verbs and Specific Nouns Important?	What Are Published Examples of Strong Verbs and Specific Nouns?
Strong verbs express actions in ways that readers can easily understand. Specific nouns are nouns that are concrete, clear, and easy for readers to visualize.	Strong Verb Examples: Sprinted Shouted Devoured Specific Noun Examples: Hockey Pizza Hawk	Strong verbs and specific nouns are important because they allow writers to express information clearly and precisely. Without them, writing would be more general and harder to understand.	Published Example of Strong Verb: "Mama **rummages** through her dresser drawer" (Williams, 2019, p. 8). Published Example of Specific Noun: "I asked him about the big **skyscrapers**…" (Warga, 2021, p. 3).

Figure 7.3.7 Strong Verb and Specific Noun Review Information

Copyright material from Sean Ruday (2025), *Grammar Toolkit Lesson Plans for Middle School*, Routledge

Graphic Organizers from Lesson 7.4: Shades of Meaning: Connotation and Denotation

Word Pairs	Denotations	Connotations
Daring and Reckless	Daring and reckless have similar denotations because they both can be used to relate to boldness and fearlessness.	Daring has a positive connotation—it is often used to describe a brave action or person. Reckless has a negative connotation—it is often used to describe someone who acts in irresponsible ways.
Leisurely and Slow	Leisurely and slow have similar denotations because they both can be used to refer to something that is done in an unhurried way.	Leisurely has a positive connotation—it is often used to refer to something done in a relaxed way that is enjoyable. Slow has a negative connotation—it often refers to something that seems to take an especially long time.

Figure 7.4.1 Word Pairs with Similar Denotations but Different Connotations

Grammatical Concepts	What Is Connotation?	What Is Denotation?	Why Is Understanding Connotation and Denotation Important?
Connotation and denotation	The connotation of a word is the association we have with that word, such as a positive, negative, or neutral tone that we connect with it.	The denotation of a word is its definition or literal meaning.	Understanding a word's connotation and denotation is important because this knowledge helps us select the word that best goes with the message and tone we want to express when writing.

Figure 7.4.2 Connotation and Denotation Information

Original Text	Revised Version with a Word with a Different Connotation
"Moo nodded at an **abandoned** Exxon station" (Erskine, 2012, p. 20).	Moo nodded at an **empty** Exxon station.

Figure 7.4.3 Original Text vs. Revised Version with Different Connotation

Copyright material from Sean Ruday (2025), *Grammar Toolkit Lesson Plans for Middle School*, Routledge

Reflection Question One	Reflection Question Two
How do you think the sentences are different?	Why do you think the author used the word abandoned in the original sentence?

Figure 7.4.4 Connotation Reflection Graphic Organizer

Grammatical Concepts	What Are Connotation and Denotation?	Why Is Understanding Connotation and Denotation Important?	Published Text Containing Language with a Specific Connotation	Revised Version with a Word with a Different Connotation but Similar Denotation
Connotation and Denotation	The **connotation** of a word is the association we have with that word, such as a positive, negative, or neutral tone. The **denotation** of a word is its definition or literal meaning.	Understanding a word's connotation and denotation is important because this knowledge helps us select the word that best goes with the message and tone we want to express when writing.	"Moo nodded at an **abandoned** Exxon station" (Erskine, 2012, p. 20).	Moo nodded at an **empty** Exxon station.

Figure 7.4.5 Connotation and Denotation Review Information

Copyright material from Sean Ruday (2025), *Grammar Toolkit Lesson Plans for Middle School*, Routledge

Graphic Organizers from Lesson 7.5: Purposeful Sentence Construction: Simple, Compound, and Complex Sentences

Sentence Type	Description	Example	Importance to Effective Writing
Simple sentence	A simple sentence is made up of one independent clause.	Kate ran the race.	Simple sentences are important to effective writing because they express information directly and clearly.

Figure 7.5.1 Key Information about Simple Sentences

Sentence Type	Description	Examples	Importance to Effective Writing
Compound sentence	A compound sentence is made up of two or more independent clauses joined by a coordinator, such as a comma and coordinating conjunction or a semicolon.	Kate ran the race, and Jake cheered her on. Kate ran the race; Jake cheered her on.	Compound sentences are important to effective writing because they connect ideas and help the flow of a piece of writing.

Figure 7.5.2 Key Information about Compound Sentences

Sentence Type	Description	Example	Importance to Effective Writing
Complex sentence	A complex sentence is made up of an independent clause and at least one dependent clause.	Since she ran the race, Kate was very tired.	Complex sentences are important to effective writing because the background information and context they provide helps the reader's understanding.

Figure 7.5.3 Key Information about Complex Sentences

Published Simple Sentence Example	Published Compound Sentence Example	Published Complex Sentence Example
"We woke up at a little before seven" (Hiranandani, 2018, p. 1). From *The Night Diary* by Veera Hiranandani	"The diner's packed with families tonight, so the show should be a hoot" (Crowder, 2022, p. 4). From *Mazie* by Melanie Crowder	"When they got close to the ramp, Papa hunkered down behind the last of the crates" (Gratz, 2017, p. 37). From *Refugee* by Alan Gratz

Figure 7.5.4 Published Examples of Simple, Compound, and Complex Sentences

Copyright material from Sean Ruday (2025), *Grammar Toolkit Lesson Plans for Middle School*, Routledge

Simple Sentence Mentor Text	Benefits of Using This Sentence Type
"We woke up at a little before seven" (Hiranandani, 2018, p. 1).	

Figure 7.5.5 Simple Sentence Benefits Analysis Chart

Compound Sentence Mentor Text	Benefits of Using This Sentence Type
"The diner's packed with families tonight, so the show should be a hoot" (Crowder, 2022, p. 4).	

Figure 7.5.6 Compound Sentence Benefits Analysis Chart

Complex Sentence Mentor Text	Benefits of Using This Sentence Type
"When they got close to the ramp, Papa hunkered down behind the last of the crates" (Gratz, 2017, p. 37).	

Figure 7.5.7 Complex Sentence Benefits Analysis Chart

Copyright material from Sean Ruday (2025), *Grammar Toolkit Lesson Plans for Middle School*, Routledge

Sentence Type	Description	Published Example	Importance to Effective Writing
Simple sentence	A simple sentence is made up of one independent clause.	"We woke up at a little before seven" (Hiranandani, 2018, p. 1).	Simple sentences are important to effective writing because they express information directly and clearly.
Compound sentence	A compound sentence is made up of two or more independent clauses joined by a coordinator, such as a comma and coordinating conjunction or a semicolon.	"The diner's packed with families tonight, so the show should be a hoot" (Crowder, 2022, p. 4).	Compound sentences are important to effective writing because they connect ideas and help the flow of a piece of writing.
Complex sentence	A complex sentence is made up of an independent clause and at least one dependent clause.	"When they got close to the ramp, Papa hunkered down behind the last of the crates" (Gratz, 2017, p. 37).	Complex sentences are important to effective writing because the background information and context they provide helps the reader's understanding.

Figure 7.5.8 Simple, Compound, and Complex Sentence Review Information

Graphic Organizers from Lesson 8.1: Purposeful Structures: Active and Passive Voices

Sentence Types	Descriptions	Examples	Why They're Used
Active voice	The subject of the sentence is performing the action.	Rob fixed the computer.	The active voice puts more emphasis on the person or thing performing the action.
Passive voice	The subject is not performing the action. The subject is the person or thing on which the action was performed.	The computer was fixed by Rob.	The passive voice focuses more on the action that was performed and the thing impacted by the action.

Figure 8.1.1 Active and Passive Voice Information

Published Active Voice Example	Published Passive Voice Example
"I stuff the note deep into my pocket" (Oh, 2021, p. 6). From *XOXO* by Axie Oh	"The article was written" (Le, 2021, p. 348). From *A Pho Love Story* by Loan Le

Figure 8.1.2 Published Examples of the Active and Passive Voices

Copyright material from Sean Ruday (2025), *Grammar Toolkit Lesson Plans for Middle School*, Routledge

Appendix B: Reproducible Graphic Organizers ◆ 213

Active Voice Mentor Text	Rewritten in Passive Voice	Passive Voice Mentor Text	Rewritten in Active Voice
"I stuff the note deep into my pocket" (Oh, 2021, p. 6).	The note is stuffed deep into my pocket by me. Or: The note is stuffed deep into my pocket.	"The article was written" (Le, 2021, p. 348).	Someone wrote the article.

Figure 8.1.3 Active and Passive Voice Mentor Texts Compared with Revised Versions

Reflection Question One	Reflection Question Two
What is a benefit of using the active voice in the active voice mentor text?	What is a benefit of using the passive voice in the passive voice mentor text?

Figure 8.1.4 Active and Passive Voice Reflection Graphic Organizer

Sentence Types	Descriptions	Published Mentor Text Examples	Why They're Used
Active voice	The subject of the sentence is performing the action.	"I stuff the note deep into my pocket" (Oh, 2021, p. 6).	The active voice puts more emphasis on the person or thing performing the action.
Passive voice	The subject is not performing the action. The subject is the person or thing on which the action was performed.	"The article was written" (Le, 2021, p. 348).	The passive voice focuses more on the action that was performed and the thing impacted by the action.

Figure 8.1.5 Active and Passive Voice Review Information

Copyright material from Sean Ruday (2025), *Grammar Toolkit Lesson Plans for Middle School*, Routledge

Graphic Organizers from Lesson 8.2: Time for a Break: Punctuation that Indicates a Pause or Break

Punctuation Mark	Used in a Sentence to Indicate a Pause or Break
Comma	After months of waiting, I finally downloaded the new album.
Dash	The new album—an amazing collection of songs—was exactly what I wanted.
Ellipsis	I finished listening to the album…and then listened to it again.

Figure 8.2.1 Examples of Punctuation Used to Indicate a Pause or Break

Grammatical Concept	What Is It?	What Are Some Punctuation Marks Used for this Purpose?	Why Is it Important?
Punctuation used to indicate a pause or break	Punctuation that writers use to show readers that they should briefly pause or break in a sentence while reading.	Comma (,) Dash (–) Ellipsis (…)	This concept is important to good writing because it helps readers understand what they're reading and allows them to read the work in the way the writer intended.

Figure 8.2.2 Key Information: Punctuation Used to Indicate a Pause or Break

Published Example of Comma Used to Indicate a Pause or Break	Published Example of a Dash Used to Indicate a Pause or Break	Published Example of an Ellipsis Used to Indicate a Pause or Break
"They didn't need to talk, which was perfect" (Emezi, 2019, p. 5). From *Pet* by Akwaeke Emezi	"But her good intentions are eclipsed by my anger and her betrayal–a dangerous combination" (Jean, 2022, p. 26). From *Tokyo Ever After* by Emiko Jean	"Are we going to…break up soon?" (Morris, 2022, p. 24). From *The Cost of Knowing* by Brittney Morris

Figure 8.2.3 Published Examples of Punctuation Used to Indicate a Pause or Break

Original Text	Revised Version that Doesn't Use a Comma to Indicate a Pause or Break
"They didn't need to talk, which was perfect" (Emezi, 2019, p. 5).	They didn't need to talk which was perfect.

Figure 8.2.4 Comma Mentor Text Compared with Revised Version

Copyright material from Sean Ruday (2025), *Grammar Toolkit Lesson Plans for Middle School*, Routledge

Appendix B: Reproducible Graphic Organizers ◆ 215

How Is Your Experience Reading the Sentence with a Comma Different from Reading the One that Does Not Contain a Comma?

Figure 8.2.5 Comma Reflection Question Graphic Organizer

Original Text	**Revised Version that Doesn't Use a Dash to Indicate a Pause or Break**
"But her good intentions are eclipsed by my anger and her betrayal–a dangerous combination" (Jean, 2022, p. 26).	But her good intentions are eclipsed by my anger and her betrayal a dangerous combination.

Figure 8.2.6 Dash Mentor Text Compared with Revised Version

How Is Your Experience Reading the Sentence with a Dash Different from Reading the One that Does Not Contain a Dash?

Figure 8.2.7 Dash Reflection Question Graphic Organizer

Original Text	**Revised Version that Doesn't Use an Ellipsis to Indicate a Pause or Break**
"Are we going to…break up soon?" (Morris, 2022, p. 24).	Are we going to break up soon?

Figure 8.2.8 Ellipsis Mentor Text Compared with Revised Version

Copyright material from Sean Ruday (2025), *Grammar Toolkit Lesson Plans for Middle School*, Routledge

How Is Your Experience Reading the Sentence with an Ellipsis Different from Reading the One that Does Not Contain an Ellipsis?

Figure 8.2.9 Ellipsis Reflection Question Graphic Organizer

What Does it Mean to Use Punctuation to Indicate a Pause or Break?	What Are Some Punctuation Marks Used for this Purpose?	Why Is Using Punctuation to Indicate a Pause or Break Important?	What Are Some Published Examples of Punctuation that Indicates a Pause or Break?
This is when writers use punctuation to show readers that they should briefly pause or break in a sentence while reading.	Comma (,) Dash (–) Ellipsis (…)	This concept is important to good writing because it helps readers understand what they're reading and allows them to read the work in the way the writer intended.	Published example using a comma: "They didn't need to talk, which was perfect" (Emezi, 2019, p. 5) Published example using a dash: "But her good intentions are eclipsed by my anger and her betrayal–a dangerous combination" (Jean, 2022, p. 26). Published example using an ellipsis: "Are we going to…break up soon?" (Morris, 2022, p. 24).

Figure 8.2.10 Review Information about Punctuation that Indicates a Pause or Break

Example Sentence that Uses a Comma to Indicate a Pause or Break	Example Sentence that Uses a Dash to Indicate a Pause or Break	Example Sentence that Uses an Ellipsis to Indicate a Pause or Break
After we swam in the pool, we ate lunch.	We saw the waterslide—a huge structure next to the pool.	We slid down the waterslide… and then slid down it again.

Figure 8.2.11 Example Sentences for Writing Activity

Copyright material from Sean Ruday (2025), *Grammar Toolkit Lesson Plans for Middle School*, Routledge

Graphic Organizers from Lesson 8.3: Key Comparisons: Comparative and Superlative Degrees

Way the Comparative and Superlative Degrees Are Formed	Examples	Types of Words it Generally Applies To
Use "-er" ending for comparative and "-est" ending for superlative	Comparative: Faster Superlative: Fastest	◆ One-syllable adjectives ◆ One-syllable adverbs ◆ Two-syllable adjectives that end in -er, -ow, -le, and -y
Add "more" before the word for comparative and "most" before the word for superlative	Comparative: More talented Superlative: Most talented	◆ Two-syllable adjectives that do not end in -er, -ow, -le, and -y ◆ Two-syllable adverbs ◆ Three-syllable adjectives
Irregular formations	Comparative: Better Superlative: Best	Some words don't follow the typical structures and instead are formed in irregular ways. Some frequently used words with irregular comparative and superlative forms are good (comparative: better; superlative: best), bad (comparative: worse; superlative: worst), and many (comparative: more; superlative: most).

Figure 8.3.1 Information about Forming the Comparative and Superlative Degrees

Grammatical Concepts	Description	Ways They Can Be Formed	Why They Are Important to Good Writing
Comparative and superlative degrees	Comparative and superlative degrees are forms of adjectives and adverbs writers use to compare information. Writers use comparative degrees to compare two things and superlative degrees to compare three or more things.	Use "-er" ending for comparative and "-est" ending for superlative Add "more" before the word for comparative and "most" before the word for superlative Irregular formations	The comparative and superlative degrees are important to good writing because they help writers express comparisons and relationships in ways that readers can easily understand.

Figure 8.3.2 Comparative and Superlative Degree Key Information

Copyright material from Sean Ruday (2025), *Grammar Toolkit Lesson Plans for Middle School*, Routledge

Published Example of Comparative Degree	Published Example of Superlative Degree
"It was easier to imagine a world of possibilities, a world where literally anyone could be related to her" (Benway, 2017, p. 25). From *Far From the Tree* by Robin Benway	"Next to the city's numerous ruins, Elantine's golden tower was the oldest structure in the Empire" (Garber, 2018, p. 85). From *Legendary* by Stephanie Garber

Figure 8.3.3 Published Examples of the Comparative and Superlative Degrees

Comparative Degree Mentor Text	Why Do You Think the Use of the Comparative Degree Is Important to the Sentence?
"It was easier to imagine a world of possibilities, a world where literally anyone could be related to her" (Benway, 2017, p. 25).	

Figure 8.3.4 Comparative Degree Mentor Text and Analysis Question

Superlative Degree Mentor Text	Why Do You Think the Use of the Superlative Degree Is Important to the Sentence?
"Next to the city's numerous ruins, Elantine's golden tower was the oldest structure in the Empire" (Garber, 2018, p. 85).	

Figure 8.3.5 Superlative Degree Mentor Text and Analysis Question

Copyright material from Sean Ruday (2025), *Grammar Toolkit Lesson Plans for Middle School*, Routledge

What Are the Comparative and Superlative Degrees?	What Are Ways They Can Be Formed?	Why Are They Important to Good Writing?	What Are Some Published Examples of Them?
Comparative and superlative degrees are forms of adjectives and adverbs writers use to compare information. Writers use comparative degrees to compare two things and superlative degrees to compare three or more things.	Use "-er" ending for comparative and "-est" ending for superlative Add "more" before the word for comparative and "most" before the word for superlative Irregular formations	The comparative and superlative degrees are important to good writing because they help writers express comparisons and relationships in ways that readers can easily understand.	Published Example of Comparative Degree: "It was easier to imagine a world of possibilities, a world where literally anyone could be related to her" (Benway, 2017, p. 25). Published Example of Superlative Degree: "Next to the city's numerous ruins, Elantine's golden tower was the oldest structure in the Empire" (Garber, 2018, p. 85).

Figure 8.3.6 Comparative and Superlative Degree Review Information

Graphic Organizers from Lesson 8.4: Tools for Variety and Versatility: Using Verbals

Kind of Verbal	Gerunds	Participles	Infinitives
Description	Gerunds are "-ing" forms of verbs that function as nouns. They can appear as single works or as gerund phrases, which are phrases that start with gerunds.	Participles are verb forms that function as adjectives. There are two kinds of participles: present participles (called the "-ing" form of a verb) and past participles (called the "-en" form of a verb). Like gerunds, participles can be used as single words or as phrases that begin with them.	Infinitives are formed by combining "to" with the base form of a verb, such as "to play." Like gerunds and participles, infinitives can be used as single words or to begin phrases. Infinitives can function as nouns, adjectives, or adverbs, depending on how they're used in a sentence.
Examples	**Swimming** is her favorite activity. ("Swimming" is a gerund.) **Swimming in the ocean** is her favorite activity. ("Swimming in the ocean" is a gerund phrase.)	**Waving**, they welcomed everyone to the party. ("Waving" is a present participle.) **Waving to the crowd**, they welcomed everyone to the party. ("Waving to the crowd" is a participial phrase that begins with a past participle.)	**To graduate** is her goal. ("To graduate" is an infinitive.) **To graduate from college** is her goal. ("To graduate from college" is an infinitive phrase.)

Figure 8.4.1 Kinds of Verbals

Grammatical Concept	What Are Verbals?	What Are Examples of Verbals?	Why Are Verbals Important to Writing?
Verbals	Verbals are grammatical concepts that are formed using verbs but function as other parts of speech, such as nouns, adjectives, or adverbs. The three kinds of verbals are gerunds, participles, and infinitives.	Gerund example: I enjoy **cooking**. Participle example: We met the **smiling** host. Infinitive example: They want **to win**.	Verbals are important to writing because they provide writers with flexibility that helps them express information in clear and accurate ways. When writers use verbals, they can use verb forms as adjectives, adverbs, or nouns.

Figure 8.4.2 Verbal Information

Copyright material from Sean Ruday (2025), *Grammar Toolkit Lesson Plans for Middle School*, Routledge

Published Gerund Example	Published Participle Example	Published Infinitive Example
"For a moment, I considered **hiding behind the wall** in the hopes that my aunt would mistake what she'd seen" (Rigaud, 2022, p. 5). From A Girl's Guide to Love and Magic by Debbie Rigaud **Hiding behind the wall** is a gerund phrase in this passage.	"The tracks push westward, the **setting** sun gilding the hillsides" (Sabic-El-Rayess, 2020, p. 3). From *The Cat I Never Named* by Amra Sabic-El-Rayess **Setting** is a participle in this passage.	"Maybe he doesn't want **to be a doctor**" (Yoon, 2016, p. 30). From The Sun Is Also A Star by Nicola Yoon **To be a doctor** is an infinitive phrase in this passage.

Figure 8.4.3 Published Examples of Verbals

Gerund Mentor Text	Analysis Question: Why Is the Gerund Important to the Sentence?
"For a moment, I considered **hiding behind the wall** in the hopes that my aunt would mistake what she'd seen" (Rigaud, 2022, p. 5).	

Figure 8.4.4 Gerund Mentor Text and Analysis Question

Participle Mentor Text	Analysis Question: Why Is the Participle Important to the Sentence?
"The tracks push westward, the **setting** sun gilding the hillsides" (Sabic-El-Rayess, 2020, p. 3).	

Figure 8.4.5 Participle Mentor Text and Analysis Question

Copyright material from Sean Ruday (2025), *Grammar Toolkit Lesson Plans for Middle School*, Routledge

Infinitive Mentor Text	Analysis Question: Why Is the Infinitive Important to the Sentence?
"Maybe he doesn't want **to be a doctor**" (Yoon, 2016, p. 30).	

Figure 8.4.6 Infinitive Mentor Text and Analysis Question

What Are Verbals?	What Are Examples of Verbals?	Why Are Verbals Important to Writing?	What Are Published Examples of Verbals?
Verbals are grammatical concepts that are formed using verbs but function as other parts of speech, such as nouns, adjectives, or adverbs. The three kinds of verbals are gerunds, participles, and infinitives.	Gerund example: I enjoy **cooking**. Participle example: We met the **smiling** host. Infinitive example: They want **to win**.	Verbals are important to writing because they provide writers with flexibility that helps them express information in clear and accurate ways. When writers use verbals, they can use verb forms as adjectives, adverbs, or nouns.	Published Gerund Example: "For a moment, I considered **hiding behind the wall** in the hopes that my aunt would mistake what she'd seen" (Rigaud, 2022, p. 5). Published Participle Example: "The tracks push westward, the **setting** sun gilding the hillsides" (Sabic-El-Rayess, 2020, p. 3). Published Infinitive Example: "Maybe he doesn't want **to be a doctor**" (Yoon, 2016, p. 56).

Figure 8.4.7 Review Information about Verbals

Gerund Example	Participle Example	Infinitive Example
They love **dancing.**	We heard the **barking** dog.	I want to swim.

Figure 8.4.8 Verbal Examples

Appendix B: Reproducible Graphic Organizers ♦ 223

Reflection Questions	Why Is the Gerund You Used Important to the Sentence in Which You Used It?	Why Is the Participle You Used Important to the Sentence in Which You Used It?	Why Is the Infinitive You Used Important to the Sentence in Which You Used It?
Your Answers			

Figure 8.4.9 Reflection Questions

Reflection Questions	Why Is the Gerund You Used Important to the Sentence in Which You Used It?	Why Is the Participle You Used Important to the Sentence in Which You Used It?	Why Is the Infinitive You Used Important to the Sentence in Which You Used It?
Your Answers	The gerund "dancing" is important to the sentence "They love dancing" because it clearly expresses what they love doing.	The participle "barking" is important to the sentence "We heard the barking dog" because it provides descriptive information about the dog.	The infinitive "to swim" is important to the sentence "I want to swim" because it tells readers exactly what the speaker wants to do.

Figure 8.4.10 Reflection Question Answer Examples

Copyright material from Sean Ruday (2025), *Grammar Toolkit Lesson Plans for Middle School*, Routledge

Graphic Organizers from Lesson 8.5: The Many Moods: The Indicative, Imperative, Interrogative, Conditional, and Subjunctive Verb Moods

Verb Moods	Descriptions	Examples
Indicative	The indicative mood makes a statement.	This is my favorite song.
Imperative	The imperative mood makes a command.	Walk the dog.
Interrogative	The interrogative mood asks a question.	Did she read the book?
Conditional	The conditional mood is used when an action is dependent on something else. It shows the condition needed for something to happen.	If I finish my homework, I will go to the game.
Subjunctive	The subjunctive mood is used to express a wish or recommendation, or to describe something that is not reality. There are two main ways the subjunctive is used: (1) In a statement that makes a recommendation, and (2) In a statement describing something that is not reality.	1. I suggest that you read this book. 2. If I were a narwhal, I would have a majestic horn.

Figure 8.5.1 Verb Mood Information

Indicative Mood Example	Imperative Mood Example	Interrogative Mood Example	Conditional Mood Example	Subjunctive Mood Example
"The Sinclairs are athletic, tall, and handsome" (Lockhart, 2018, p. 3). From *We Were Liars* by E. Lockhart	"Help her!" (Collins, 2020, p. 188). From The Ballad of Songbirds and Snakes by Suzanne Collins	"How does this woman know my name?" (Colbert, 2019, p. 2). From The Revolution of Birdie Randolph by Brandy Colbert	"'Let's wait and see if the kid survives the beach landing,' Big John said. 'Then we can worry about a nickname for him'" (Gratz, 2018, p. 15). From *Grenade* by Alan Gratz	"If they knew anything about us, they'd know you can't perform in that" (Allen, 2023, p. 2). From *All You Have to Do* by Autumn Allen

Figure 8.5.2 Published Verb Mood Examples

Verb Mood	Mentor Text	Why the Verb Mood Is Important to the Example's Effectiveness
Indicative	"The Sinclairs are athletic, tall, and handsome" (Lockart, 2018, p. 3).	
Imperative	"Help her!" (Collins, 2020, p. 188).	
Interrogative	"How does this woman know my name?" (Colbert, 2019, p. 2).	
Conditional	"'Let's wait and see if the kid survives the beach landing,' Big John said. 'Then we can worry about a nickname for him'" (Gratz, 2018, p. 15).	
Subjunctive	"If they knew anything about us, they'd know you can't perform in that" (Allen, 2023, p. 2).	

Figure 8.5.3 Verb Mood Mentor Text Analysis Chart

For Product Safety Concerns and Information please contact our EU
representative GPSR@taylorandfrancis.com
Taylor & Francis Verlag GmbH, Kaufingerstraße 24, 80331 München, Germany

www.ingramcontent.com/pod-product-compliance
Lightning Source LLC
Chambersburg PA
CBHW081147230426
43664CB00018B/2833